Praise for *Where T...*

T0015200

"Ever a reliable source of grace, Heather Plett once again offers a sunlit window into the process of healing. *Where Tenderness Lives* is an honest-to-the-bones chronicling of a woman's metamorphosis in a patriarchal culture, turning the pain and shame of trauma into joyful, embodied freedom. This is the kind of inspiration that lifts all women."

BECKY VOLLMER, author of *You Are Not Stuck*

"To tell our stories is brave and beautiful, especially those we'd prefer to forget. Heather Plett does this with vulnerability and grace. Though her experiences are distinctly hers, she tenderly and brilliantly invites us into our own, offering profound healing and hope along the way."

RONNA DETRICK, author of *Rewriting Eve*

"Some people write their stories to heal themselves. Others write their stories to heal others. Heather Plett does both. Poignant and powerful, Heather delivers a can't-put-down book of struggle and suffering, but also resilience and joy. She shows that holding space for yourself is the first and most important step on the road to your healing and freedom."

DAVID HAYWARD, aka NakedPastor

"Story has never been more important for our communal healing, and Heather Plett is one of the greatest impact-to-action storytellers of our time. Her writing has helped me grieve and grow while expanding my understanding of how to be a better leader, partner, and friend."

MARK BRAND, social impact entrepreneur, chef, and host of *Better*

"Through Heather Plett's incredibly rich and deeply personal life stories, which she shares so articulately, there were multiple opportunities for me to learn and apply her insights to my own life. Her reflections made me consider some big questions about how I want to be in the world—and how I want the world to be. My heart has been touched and I am inspired for my own growth journey."

"This powerful, piercing assemblage of turning-point stories from Heather Plett—as daughter, wife, mother, survivor, teacher, and abolitionist—casts a wide lens beyond her personal experiences to the oppressive systems that shape societal harm. Heather invites the reader to do their own liberatory work, and in doing so, is handing us a key to liberate our own unhealed stories."

"Bravely, beautifully, Heather Plett takes us on a journey into her life. We go along gladly, for every bit of her hard-won growth and wisdom is absolutely genuine, and generous too. Journeying with her takes us into our own lives as well, to consider our upbringing, our relationships, our bodies, our pain. Best of all, this wonderful guide moves us through struggle into the warm embrace of tenderness, courage, and joy."

"As Heather Plett leads with her stories—vulnerably, powerfully—and holds a beautiful, tender space for herself first, she invites us to do the same. I was deeply moved by this book."

ON HEALING, LIBERATION,
AND HOLDING SPACE FOR ONESELF

WHERE TENDERNESS LIVES

heather plett

PAGE TWO

Cataloguing in publication information is
available from Library and Archives Canada.
ISBN 978-1-77458-363-0 (paperback)
ISBN 978-1-77458-364-7 (ebook)

Page Two
pagetwo.com

Edited by Kendra Ward
Copyedited by Melissa Kawaguchi
Proofread by Alison Strobel
Cover and interior design by Taysia Louie
Printed and bound in Canada by Friesens
Distributed in Canada by Raincoast Books
Distributed in the US and internationally by Macmillan

24 25 26 27 28   5 4 3 2 1

heatherplett.com

I dedicate this book to you, dear reader,
and I dedicate it to me.
I dedicate it to our ongoing efforts to be healed
and whole, liberated and tender.

Contents

Preface

SEVERAL YEARS AGO, while I was preparing for a trip to Ethiopia, where I'd be spending time with some of the most marginalized people in the world, a friend who lived there recommended I read *Man's Search for Meaning* by Viktor Frankl. "You'll be seeing some hard things," Sam said. "The book will help you make sense of what you're seeing."

In the years since, that book has helped me reshape the hard things in my life into stories with meaning, and that meaning has helped me wake up the next day and carry on. Since then, I've also learned, from the work of psychiatrist and writer Dr. Dan Siegel, that writing and rewriting our stories of pain until we can make a cohesive narrative of them helps us heal the trauma that is held within those stories and step into new stories. I have known this intuitively since I was in my early twenties when I wrote a play about a sexual assault I suffered, but it was good to have it validated by an expert.

On these pages, you will find many such stories from my life. They have all been written and rewritten many times in my journal, and then, eventually, they evolved into something worth sharing. I offer them to you because of something else I've learned along the way—that healing becomes even richer when the sharing of it invites other people into their own healing. While solitary healing is wonderful, collective healing adds a whole other level of beauty and possibility to the mix, for all involved.

As Joni Mitchell has said of her songs, "If you listen to that music and you see me, you're not getting anything out of it. If you listen to that music and you see yourself, it will probably make you cry, and you'll learn something about yourself and now you're getting something out of it." I hope that when you read these stories, you will see yourself in them, even if that makes you cry. I hope that you will feel like you have a friend, walking alongside you, telling you stories and giving you love and encouragement (and perhaps passing you a tissue when you need it) as you do your own work to heal and grow and become more liberated and tender.

For that purpose, to help you feel more like you've found a new friend, at the end of each chapter to follow, I've shared reflection questions meant to help you with your own exploration. You can pause after each chapter for contemplation, or you can read the book cover to cover and then pull out your journal for some intensive personal reflection time. Alternatively, you can use the questions to spark conversations with your book club or sharing circle if you choose this book (which I hope you do).

While I hope this book offers healing, my even bolder hope is that it invites liberation. Healing is only part of the story, because if we only heal what has hurt us personally but never address the systemic nature of that harm, then the harm will continue in perpetuity, to others if not to us. That's why I have tried, in most of these stories, to be more expansive, to invite reflection of the bigger narrative beyond my personal narrative. Sometimes that narrative is complex and hard to pin down, which is why it's often easier to simply look at the individual narratives within it, but I have a bigger dream than just my own healing and liberation. I have a dream of collective liberation and the co-creation of better ways of being together. This book is about that, too.

One last thing... telling stories like this is sometimes challenging because other people are in the stories, and while I write to heal, liberate, and alchemize whatever wounding might have happened in the stories, I don't want to be the cause of anyone else's pain. I have tried as diligently as I could to be fair to all the people whose lives have been intertwined with mine over the years, and to tell these stories with integrity and compassion, but there were times when I had to make some difficult choices in order to be honest about my own life. In the end, I chose to be true to myself, to be—first and foremost—as honest as I could be about my own role in those stories, and, finally, not to abandon myself by leaving the hardest parts of my stories out.

Each of us has a different perception of reality, and if you were to hear any of these stories from others who were part of them, you would hear different stories. In the end, the "truth" of those stories becomes less relevant than the impact those stories have on each of us and the ways in which we choose to integrate them into our lives. It is my intention, always, to tell stories in a way that allows each person in them to seek their own truth and their own healing.

Just as I have chosen to be true to myself, dear reader, I hope that you, too, are learning to be true to yourself and that these stories will serve as inspiration and companionship for you as you do so. May we all find the courage to heal, become more liberated, and hold space for ourselves. May we all have the courage to tell the truth.

With tenderness,
Heather

The Girl in the Velcro Dress

T HERE ONCE was a girl who wore a Velcro dress.

In childhood, before any other options were apparent to her, she'd stitched that dress out of bits that had been passed down by her mother and the women who came before. "It's to protect you," the women said as they taught her how to sew. "We want you to be well prepared for life." Into the stitches were woven expectations from her culture, her religion, her family system, the media, and all the adults who'd grown up with Velcro clothing of their own.

The Velcro made it easy for other people to attach things to her. Some people attached rules about how she should behave. Others attached their own needs and the pain they didn't know how to heal. Still others attached disapproval, judgment, rules about good Christian behaviour, and expectations about her body.

It was such a familiar pattern to have other people's things clinging to her dress that she began picking up pieces that shouldn't have been her responsibility, often saying yes when she wanted to say no. Under the weight of that dress, her own body became an enigma to her—just a vehicle to carry the dress around.

By the time she was a young woman, she knew no other life but the one in that dress. The dress gave her a sense of purpose, and people praised her for how much she could carry. Some called her "resilient," some called her "strong," some called her "resourceful," and some called her "godly." She gathered those words and stuck them to the dress.

A day finally came when the girl could barely breathe under the weight of the dress. Exhausted, she propped the heavy dress up like a concrete tent, slipped down into the cavity it created, curled up in a ball on the floor, and wept.

In her tiny cave under the dress, after many tears had been shed, the girl began to fantasize about what it would be like to live without that dress—about how freely she could move through the world without the weight of other people's expectations, judgments, and needs.

Guilt quickly consumed her, though, and she shook herself out of the dream. Gritting her teeth, she picked herself up off the floor, slipped back into the dress, and carried on. "I am resilient," she told herself as she struggled to stand up straight.

Once the fantasy was awakened, though, it wouldn't let go. Soon she was sneaking away regularly into her little cave, entertaining the dream that another life might be possible. While there, she noticed how different her breath felt—long and slow and filling her whole body. When she wore the dress, her breath was short and fast and a little strangled, but under the dress, it was different. Her body started to feel safe in a way that she'd never felt while wearing the dress.

The girl started to plan moments in her day when she could slip under the dress and disappear—moments that didn't inconvenience her children, her husband, her mother, her employer, or anyone else who depended on her. At first, those moments in the cave were quiet and dark, but one day, just before slipping into the cave, she grabbed her music player and took it with her. She lay on the floor of the cave with her headphones on, and soon the music filled her body with a surprising feeling of aliveness.

She wondered what else could bring on that feeling. Her journal and pen soon joined her in the cave. A new set of paintbrushes and paints came next, as did scissors and glue, and one day she worked up the courage to bring down power tools. Hidden from view from all who knew her, she felt almost childlike again, making playful messes with art supplies and wood.

One day, the girl was surprised to discover a secret doorway at the bottom edge of the cave. It made her nervous at first, but when she worked up the courage to crawl through that doorway, she found a magical room that reminded her of the images from magazines of retreat centres and healing spaces that she'd pasted onto collages in her secret cave. The discovery both delighted and frightened her. There were other people there, but she was reluctant to join them at first, fearing she might shame herself or be too exposed. She scurried back to her own cave, closing the door behind her and slipping quickly back into the dress.

Her curiosity soon got the better of her, though, and a few weeks later, she crept quietly back through the door into the magical room. She made her body as small as she could at the edge of the space, hoping nobody would notice her.

With time, though, after lots of people had smiled at her and she felt ready to trust them, she moved a little further into the room. She discovered that the room held the most interesting mix of people she'd ever come across—misfits, artists, dancers, dreamers, and revolutionaries. They all seemed to share that same aliveness that had come over her body when she'd found what most delighted her back in her own cave. Some of their activity was similar to what she did in her cave, but they were doing other things, too, like clustering in circles for healing conversations, dancing with each other, and gathering around markers and poster boards making protest signs. Gradually, as the girl's courage kindled, she joined in and expanded her experimentation—this time in the company of other people— with the things that made her feel alive. Sometimes, while she was lost in the act of creating, she had flashbacks to how she'd felt in childhood before her dress got so heavy.

BACK IN her own cave, spurred on by the courage she witnessed in the magical room, the girl grew bolder with her art-making, and soon the inside of her cave was covered in paint. Fanciful creatures and shapes danced across the walls in colourful, messy glee. It was beginning to feel like a home she wanted to live in.

The transformation inside the dress soon started to impact the outside of the dress as well. Gaining courage from her time in the cave and in the magical room, the girl became curious about whether she could peel anything off her dress. She grabbed the first things she could find—an old belief about what good girls should wear in public—peeled it away and dropped it on the floor. It bounced back and tried to reattach itself, but she peeled it off repeatedly until it lost all stickiness and stayed on the floor. That gave her the courage to peel back another thing, and another, and each thing that dropped to the floor made her a little bolder to peel back the next.

Some of those things had to be tenderly, and sometimes cautiously, returned to the person who put them there in the first place. Those were the hardest to release, because one of the things that clung to her dress the most stubbornly was the expectation that she should never hurt anyone's feelings.

Once a few layers had been removed, she realized that the dress underneath was not as sticky as it once had been. In all those repeated peelings, she'd managed to detach some of the hooks from the Velcro. When people tried to attach new things in the empty spaces, the items simply slipped to the floor.

1

The Woman
I Needed Her to Be

Y MOM gave birth to me, her first daughter after two sons, and then she died. She didn't stay dead, but according to the doctor, who later said he felt like God when he managed to bring her back from death's door, she was as close to dead as one can be without needing a funeral. She hemorrhaged and lost so much blood that her heart assumed it had nothing to pump and stopped beating.

While she was in recovery, the nurses tried to feed me with a bottle, but I screamed and refused to drink from it. I would not be satisfied until a nurse held me over my mom's breast so that I could suckle. Mom lay helpless and unable to pull me to her, her arms strapped to the bed rails with IVs in each arm pumping blood back into her body to replace what she'd lost.

This narrative, which I heard many times growing up, represents both my formation story and the landscape in which my life has been shaped. In a lifelong quest, I have stubbornly sought a mother who could feed me, nurture me, and hold me to her breast. My mother tried to do her best but was forever held back from giving the kind of love I most longed for by invisible tethers that kept her bound.

IN MY mid-twenties, fresh out of university and dating the man I would eventually marry, I wrote and produced a play called *Poetic License*. In it, a young woman named Jeannie is working with a co-author she has hired to write the story of her life. She's writing it the way she *wants* it to happen, though, not the way it is *actually* happening. In the beginning, she creates the characters—her love interest, family, and friends—and then manipulates them to behave the way she wants them to behave. Partway through the play, the characters realize they are simply pawns in Jeannie's story and they revolt, taking control of their own lives and leaving her alone with no one left to populate her narrative.

Full of ambition and hope, I formed a small theatre company to mount that play at the Winnipeg Fringe Festival. It was one of three plays I wrote and produced in my mid-twenties, when dreams of spending my life as a writer still felt possible—before I followed the path of least resistance, got married, became a mom, and settled into a secure government job with good benefits.

"I'm too stupid to understand what was going on in that play" was my mom's response when she saw *Poetic License*. There was no praise, no affirmation of my courage or writing skills, just self-deprecation. My success somehow alchemized into her failure. I heard the same thing from her every time I had a measure of success. As though still tethered to an invisible bed, she was unable to nurture the part of me that was hungry for a mother's love and celebration in those moments. I wasn't surprised by her reaction, but it still hurt, and it still dampened the pride I felt over what I'd accomplished. It hurt, but I brushed it aside and tried, as always, to assure her that she was smarter than she gave herself credit for.

I wanted more from her. I ached for her to throw off the chains of her own insecurities and simply tell me I'd done a good job. I wanted that moment to be about me. Like Jeannie, I wanted to write a narrative in which my mom was able to meet my needs. I left the theatre deflated and still hungry.

I'VE BEEN trying for months to write about my mother but, not unlike Jeannie, I still don't know how to shape her on this page. Relegated to memory in the decade since her death, she shapeshifts, depending on the place she holds in that moment in my narrative and my healing journey. Perhaps that means that my relationship with her remains unresolved. Perhaps it means I'm still Jeannie, trying too hard to manipulate the characters in my story instead of letting them simply be who they are (or were). Perhaps it's because of my insatiable hunger.

I could write her the way she shows up in conversations with my siblings. In that shape, she baked a lot of buns and always made my brother's favourite peppermint brownies when he came home for Christmas. She toiled selflessly in the kitchen, knew each of our favourite foods, and fed us the kind of love she knew how to give, through waffles, lemon loaf, and the best chicken gravy ever known to humankind. She taught us to be grateful and generous and to gather people around us by serving whatever needs we could fill.

If you were to ask my childhood friends to describe my mom, you'd hear about how she was the most expressive storyteller in Sunday School and was one of the only grownups playful enough to start water fights at the annual church picnic. You might also hear about how welcoming our home was and how lovingly she embraced lonely and wounded people. There were the foster children who spent months in our home during their mom's repeated psychiatric-ward stays. And there were the twins who, when their dad died and their mom moved into town, needed a safe second home on a farm. And there was the woman who needed a place to hide with her children, away from her abusive husband.

All of that is true of my mom. Her heart was generous and sacrificial, and a lot of people loved her. She was a Good Christian Woman. She knew how to give Good Christian Love.

But another part of my mom is harder for me to write about because it casts some shadows on the memory of her. She was deeply insecure. She never believed she measured up to the scale of Christian goodness that she kept always outside her own reach. While she was faultlessly kind to other people, she was often unkind to herself, and she couldn't see how her low self-esteem kept her from unconditionally nurturing her children or celebrating their successes.

Mom was afraid of a lot of things. She was afraid of letting people down, afraid of people thinking ill of her, afraid of being abandoned, afraid of not being good enough, and—more than anything else—afraid of hell. She was afraid that she, or perhaps even worse, one of her children, would fall out of favour with God and be banished to an eternity in hell. This was an all-consuming fear, born at least in part because her own mom died when she was only six, and she came to believe, subconsciously, that people would abandon her. Every time I chose something different from what she thought was the path to heaven, she would become anxious and do her best to bring me back to righteousness and safety. Because she was always faultlessly kind, those efforts often landed as passive-aggressiveness.

I see it so clearly now, in ways I couldn't see it when I was growing up, how much she longed for safety and how much she feared abandonment.

IN MY basement is a Rubbermaid box full of memories. It's been filled mostly by the emptying of homes—first when Dad died and Mom moved off the farm, and then when Mom died and her second husband quickly moved on to marry his third wife. Whenever I flip through the old journals, letters, cards, playbills, and concert tickets in that box, I find pieces of my former self. Sometimes that hurts, and sometimes it heals. Sometimes it does both at once.

There are the journal entries of the young version of me who'd been raped and didn't know how to talk to her family about the darkness the rapist left behind. And there are endless poems about loneliness and despair in the years that followed—feelings I only knew how to write on the page and never speak out loud. There's an account of the time I tried but failed to go to group therapy for rape survivors, and there are countless middle-of-the-night heartaches.

"Somewhere there's a world called sleep, but I am a foreigner there."

"Thousands of people, but I am alone. Isn't it strange that in this crowd nobody hears me crying?"

"Lying alone in my room, fighting a vicious battle with my mind."

The first time I opened the box, a few years after Mom's death, the pages from the journals and letters that hurt the most were the ones that revealed how much twenty-something me longed to be seen but was afraid she'd be judged—still that infant seeking her mother's milk, and still Jeannie, trying to write characters who would meet her needs. "Mom wanted to know how I was doing," says one journal entry, in the most agonizing of those journals, written in the years following my rape. "For some reason, I just can't tell her. I just clam up when she asks me, and I don't respond. Sometimes I wish I could, because I know I'm hurting her. Why is it that sometimes I want to hurt her? Maybe because I can't stand her pious preaching. And maybe just because I like to be tough and independent. I wish I wasn't so hard on her, because she really loves me. I think I'm afraid I can't be good enough for her."

In the letters I'd sent home, there are lots of little clues about the daughter who wanted to be found worthy, to have her mother break the chains and hold her close. "I hope you don't think I'm sinful, but I enjoy ballet," said one. And in another, a faltering attempt at apology for occasional consumption of alcoholic beverages. Dance and drink—two of the forbidden fruits of the Mennonite worldview that kept my mom bound.

And then there were the letters from Mom to me; in nearly every one was a plea for more godliness. "I don't want to appear like a preaching mom, but if only I could know that walking with the Lord was as important to you as your career, etc., you would make me a very very happy mom. Never forget that we are here to magnify the Lord and somehow I get the feeling maybe you are not really victorious. I hope I'm wrong." And another: "Heather, please don't think I have ever doubted that you were a Christian. I've never thought that. I'm just concerned. It's so important we live for the Lord and I'm sure you're doing that, maybe even more than I do. I fail so often, at work and with Dad, so please pray for me too."

Perhaps most painful is the journal page with "To Mom and Dad" written across the top.

Why is it that the more satisfied I am with myself, the more disappointed you seem to be in me? It seems you don't understand me anymore, since I left. I know I've changed, but didn't you expect that? I couldn't always be your good little girl. I had to experience life on my own. Sure I've made some mistakes and I still do, but can't you forgive me for that? Can't you accept the fact that I've chosen a different lifestyle from yours? Look at me. I'm not really so bad and I do still love you, though I do some of the things you always told me not to. That's because I want to know if they're really wrong or if that's just the tradition. You didn't always have reasons for the things you told me not to do, so I want to know if there really are reasons. So forgive me. And love me anyway.

"Look at me." Those words jump from the page, and I whisper to that twenty-something woman, "I'm looking at you now."

I WAS in the playground with my friends at Arden Elementary School, a small square box of a school in our tiny town, when a car sped into the parking lot and came to an abrupt halt at the front door. The driver—my friend Lisa's mom—erupted from the car, slammed the door, and marched into the school. Those of us watching snickered, because we knew that she was there, as she had been before, to yell at a teacher for disciplining one of her sons.

Why does that random memory still hold in a mind that has wiped out so many of the details of my childhood? Because I was dumbfounded that a parent would stand up for their child like that. I suppose I wanted that but knew I couldn't count on the same from my parents. Both pacifism and respect for (or fear of) authority ran deeply in our belief system, so if my siblings or I ever got into trouble at school (which we very rarely did), nobody would show up to defend us. It would simply be assumed that the person in authority was right.

Several years later, when I was in my early twenties and had just driven home from the city to tell my parents that the night before I'd been violently raped, I was amazed by my dad's response. At first, he simply walked out of the house to the barn, hunched over and speechless. When he came back, he told me a story of a man he knew who'd spent much of his life hunting down the man who'd raped his daughter. "Now I understand how he felt," Dad said. My pacifist father, who I'd never known to raise a hand against anyone, was considering how he could hurt another man on my behalf. That was one of the most loving things I ever heard my dad say.

My childhood home felt safe, but, after many sessions with a therapist, I've come to see just how unprotected I felt as a child and how much I, like my mom, longed for safety. Neither would I be defended, nor did I learn to defend myself, when harm came to me. Turning the other cheek was the way of my people, and so I turned and turned and turned again, never looking back to see whether anyone was standing up for me and never believing in my right to stand up for myself. The infant whose mother's arms couldn't wrap around her didn't trust that those arms would be there to keep her from harm.

When a woman who'd been victimized by domestic violence came to our house with her children when I was a young teenager, my parents offered her safety for a few weeks, and then invited her abuser into our living room and negotiated a truce between them. By the time we children were allowed back into the living room, the abused woman was sitting in her abuser's lap. At the end of the day, we stood at the window and watched abuser and abused go home together, their small children in tow. That was the way of peace. That was a cheek successfully turned. Forgive and forget, abuse victims were told.

A FEW YEARS AGO, after both of my parents had died, and not long after I finally chose to stop turning the other cheek and ended my own marriage, I was confronted with the painful realization that not only had I been blindly living in that belief system, but I'd also passed it on to my children. Even though I'd convinced myself that I was parenting differently, I had been doing the same thing my mom and dad had done. I'd left my own daughters feeling undefended, and I'd taught them to accept abusive behaviour.

Two things happened in quick succession, and it all felt uncomfortably clear.

First, my middle daughter, Julie, who was in therapy at the time, let me know how much she was wrestling with a feeling of betrayal because she didn't believe I had protected her from her father's emotional abuse in her teen years. I reacted defensively at first, not wanting to believe her version of the story, because I recalled many horrible moments during her teenage years when I'd gotten between her and her dad, especially when he picked fights with her for no apparent reason. But keeping the peace wasn't the same as protecting—I was simply leaning back on my pacifist roots and teaching her to turn the other cheek with her dad.

To suddenly find out that Julie had grown up, like I had, believing that her mom would not protect her from harm, was devastating to me. I crawled into my bed and wept.

Second, my youngest daughter, Madeline, who had become a climate activist at the age of seventeen and was garnering considerable national media attention at the time, received an unkind direct message from an older male relative who dismissed her activism and called her a "silly girl." When she showed me the message, I had the sudden realization that I had an opportunity to change old patterns and no longer turn the other cheek when someone harmed my child. I was terrified (my nervous system kept telling me how unsafe it was to stand up to someone with seemingly more authority), but I was also enraged and knew I had to let my daughters know that I would defend them. I sent a strongly worded message to that relative about how wrongheaded his message was and told him not to contact Madeline again. Then I blocked him on social media, finally giving myself the firm boundary I'd never seen as a possibility before. (Madeline's response to him was simple and elegant: "Ok boomer.")

A FEW YEARS after Mom died, I was still trying to make sense of her legacy in me. While the grief was intense at first, my feelings toward her kept morphing and, even with therapy, I couldn't let go of what felt like an unresolved narrative.

In the year before she died, when we already knew she had cancer and might not be with us for much longer, I agonized over whether to attempt a heart-to-heart conversation with her. "Look at me," I still wanted to say, like the twenty-something woman in that journal, and the infant seeking the breast, but... could I trust her to hold my truth without judgment? On the one hand, I might feel more at peace with her dying if I knew that I'd been truthful with her, but on the other hand... what if I hurt her and did irreparable damage to our relationship in her final days? I'd have to live with the guilt of that after she died.

I wanted to tell her about my dreams for the work I'd started two years earlier, when I left traditional employment and started my own business, but I was afraid she'd diminish those dreams with her own insecurity. I wanted to tell her about how much my marriage was faltering, but I was afraid she'd say it was because I wasn't letting God into the marriage. I wanted to tell her about my daughters coming out of the closet and about how I wasn't sure I was heterosexual myself, but I was certain she wouldn't get past her belief that it was sin. I wanted to tell her how different my faith was from hers—how I could no longer believe in an exclusively male God or many of the teachings of the church—but I knew how much her fear of hell would get in the way of her ability to hear me.

In the end, I didn't attempt that heart-to-heart. It might have been because of fear, distrust, kindness, trauma, or a genuine desire not to hurt her. It might have been all of those things combined. The truth is rarely a simple equation.

A healing fantasy—that's what psychologist Lindsay Gibson would call my aching desire to be truly seen and unconditionally loved by my mom. (I only learned the term a few years after Mom died.) A healing fantasy is the kind of hopeful story that helps a child cope in a dysfunctional family environment, where they tell themselves that something magical will happen—perhaps they'll win fame and fortune, or they'll finally become the person their parents wanted them to be, or their parents will have a miraculous change of heart—that will win them the love, belonging, and safety they crave. Perhaps it was a healing fantasy that was at the heart of that play I wrote in my twenties, about Jeannie and her attempts to line up the characters in her narrative in a way that would meet her needs. Perhaps that fantasy started the moment the nurse held me above my mother's prostrate body.

I had a glimmer of hope, at first, that I could have that heart-to-heart conversation. But one day, a few months before Mom died, I finally accepted that it was a fantasy and decided it was best to set it aside. Instead, I tried to give her what I'd always wanted from her—to see her as she was, not as I wanted her to be.

A couple of years later, though, something still felt unsettled. Whenever I thought about her, I felt the turmoil of unresolved emotions.

I decided to let the pain come to the surface, to stop sugar-coating it and really let myself feel it all, no matter how much it might damage my memory of her. I had to stop gaslighting the emotional experience of my younger self, stop telling myself I had nothing to complain about because I wasn't truly abused and my mom was always a kind and lovely person. I admitted to myself that I'd felt abandoned and unprotected, that I hadn't felt truly seen or unconditionally loved, that I'd been afraid to succeed because my success was always diminished, that I'd carried shame because I didn't live up to her expectations, that I'd almost always prioritized her emotions over my own, that I'd resented having to comfort her insecurities in the moments of my own success, that I'd let her fear control too much of my life, and that my fear of hurting her kept me from my own true life.

Hurt, betrayal, grief, anger, disappointment—all those emotions and more came to the surface, and I let them. I stopped trying to censor myself the way I'd done for so many years. I stopped excusing or justifying her behaviour. I simply let myself feel what I'd denied myself before. I stopped telling myself, "She didn't know better" or "She was simply projecting her own pain and fear onto me and didn't mean to do it" or "She didn't know how to parent me because she lost her mom at a young age." I just let all the parts of me that I'd buried in the past—the young girl in the school playground, the young woman alone in her bed, the young mom with a troublesome marriage—feel what they needed to feel. I let myself rage, flail, hurt, cry, and even blame. Mostly, I let myself long for the woman I'd needed her to be, the mother I'd been crying for since the day I was born.

I also had to grapple with one of the things that kept getting in the way of truly owning my experience—the fact that my siblings' experiences and memories of our mom are different from mine. "They might not be wrestling with the hurt I felt," I kept telling myself, "but my hurt was still real." To admit that she hadn't given me what I needed was not a betrayal of my siblings' memories of her.

WHEN JULIE confronted me about how she'd felt betrayed and unprotected by me in her teen years, I had, fortunately, already processed a lot of the pain from my own teen years. Perhaps that's why she believed she could trust me with her story.

At first, I was defensive and wanted to project the blame away from me and onto her father, but I knew that would be a mistake. Instead, I worked hard to swallow my pride, soothe the reactivity and defensiveness of my nervous system, truly listen to her, and hold space for the painful things she'd experienced and the ways I'd let her down. Then I apologized and asked her what I could do differently in the future. "Look at me," my child said, in her own words, and I did my best to look.

When that happened, and I found myself on the other side of the heart-to-heart conversation I'd once fantasized about—the mother now instead of the daughter I'd been on those journal pages—a few things happened. First, I saw more clearly what I'd longed for and rarely received. Second, I could access more empathy for my mom, knowing how hard it is to truly see a child who's asking you to witness them and take responsibility for the ways you weren't able to meet their needs. Third, something inside me was healed because I knew I was breaking the cycle and passing on a different story to the next generation of daughters.

When I learned to see my daughters in the ways I'd longed to be seen, I also learned to see myself and all the parts of me that were hidden in that Pandora's box in the basement. As I write this, in fact, that box sits in front of me, open and fully revealed.

"Look at me," the box says, and I look. I unhook my arms from the bed that held my mother, and I hold the child self that still longs for the circle of those arms.

I continue to learn new ways to mother myself at all ages, and I have also learned how to receive mothering from beloved friends and elders who have done their own healing work and know how to give healthy, unconditional love. Beyond human mothers, I have discovered that I can turn to Mother Earth, who holds me in her embrace, reaching to me with the untethered arms of trees, rivers, butterflies, and horses.

PERHAPS IT is only now, thirty years after I wrote that play (and more than fifty years after I screamed in that hospital room), that I am finally ready to set down my pen and stop trying to craft the characters in my life into who I need them to be. Mom was flawed and more complicated than what could be seen on the surface. She was, at times, insecure, fearful, passive-aggressive, and judgmental. She wasn't always the mom I needed her to be. She was afraid of my successes, afraid of the ways I didn't live righteously, and afraid to let me grow into the woman I wanted to become. She was bound by a religion and a childhood that almost always kept her small, afraid, and ashamed. She passed all that on to me. Lacking her own embodied feeling of safety, she didn't know how to give that to her children.

All those things are true . . . *and* she was also loving and kind and did the best that she could with the resources she had at the time. She was never able to see herself for who she was—a traumatized woman passing that trauma on to her children— and, under heaps of pressure in a patriarchal world to be so many things for so many people, she never got the tools or support she needed to heal or thrive. Instead, those who pumped the blood into her veins also strapped her arms to the bed. She carried her own healing fantasy, which probably formed the moment her mom died an untimely death. Instead of finding out how to heal that and free herself and the generations to come, she clung to the people she was afraid would abandon her, and she passed her pain on to those she birthed.

There is little left to say other than this:

I love you, Mom, and I forgive you. I see you. I hope that, if there is an afterlife, as you so believed there would be, you are finally free of the chains passed down through the bloodlines to you. And I hope that you feel safe and loved.

I choose to picture you, Mom, untethered and at peace, with the awareness, finally, that you and I were always worthy of love and that we didn't need to strive so hard to measure up. I imagine you watching your children and grandchildren now with new eyes, sending us healing and unconditional love, hoping that we will learn to be free before death knocks on our doors.

When my mom was dying, birds began to appear at meaningful moments, forever attaching themselves to my memory of that time. When Mom could do little else but sit and stare out the window, she became enamoured with the birds that would come to the feeders her husband had hung on the deck railing just outside her window. I bought her a bird book to help her identify those birds, but I don't think she ever opened it. She didn't need to know what they were; she just wanted to watch them.

A few days before Mom died, when my sister and I were driving to visit her, an eagle sat on a tree not far from her home, watching us like a sentry guarding the gate to a sacred place. Then, shortly after Mom's spirit left her body, a beautiful woodpecker appeared at one of the feeders she'd once enjoyed watching.

In the long days of vigil that led to her dying, I sat at her bedside and read the book *When Women Were Birds*. In it, Terry Tempest Williams writes about how she'd inherited her mother's journals and had been instructed by her not to open them until after her mother's death. When Williams finally opened them, she found all the journals empty. In the book, she speculates about the message of those empty journals, passed to her by a mother whose voice had been silenced much of her life. In a sense, my mom left me her own empty journals, and, without the benefit of ever knowing her true voice, I am left trying to make meaning of the empty pages.

Now I often think of my mom when birds appear, especially when those birds are eagles or woodpeckers. I like to picture her, somewhere beyond the bounds of her human life, flying free, finally untethered and singing in an uninhibited voice.

REFLECTION QUESTIONS

THIS CHAPTER IS about my relationship with my mom, but in your exploration, consider any relationship that might have shaped you in your early years. We all emerged from the womb longing for love and attachment from the people who were responsible for our care. Sometimes those people were able to meet those needs and sometimes they weren't. As those of us who have since become parents know, every person carries their own wounds into their parenting role, and so nobody can live up to the parenting ideals we have in our heads. Many of us carry residual wounds that we need to find ways to heal in our adult lives.

1   What are you experiencing now that might be attached to childhood needs that weren't met?

2   In the journal from my early adulthood, the words "look at me" jumped off the page. If you reflect on your teen years or early adulthood, who did you most long to be seen by?

3   Safety and belonging are two of the most basic needs of any human. How were those needs met or not met in your childhood? What are you doing now to meet those needs for yourself?

4   In the story, I share how, in order to heal, I needed to let myself feel the hurt and anger I could not express in my earlier years. Which emotions might you have denied yourself that you now need to hold space for?

5   Love is complicated. Although I loved my mother dearly, I also needed to acknowledge her flaws so that I could heal the wounds left behind in me and choose my own way forward. What messages do you carry about what you're not allowed to say to, or about, the people you love?

6   How can you hold space for your younger self who still feels some of the pain from earlier parts of your life?

7   If you could write a letter to the person who wasn't able to meet your needs in childhood, what would you say?

2

His Hands at My Throat

"THERE'S A tightening in my throat," I told my therapist. "It shows up when I'm anxious or ashamed or when there is conflict and I am afraid to speak. It blocks my voice and makes it hard to breathe. It's been worse than ever lately."

By this time, I'd learned a lot about trauma and how it can settle into your body when you aren't supported in processing and releasing distressing events in your life (especially if those events happened when you were young and you didn't know how to put them into context). I had experimented with healing modalities—talk therapy, somatic healing, and several practices on the fringes of both. I'd excavated and healed, and excavated and healed some more. Many times, I thought that I'd found and dealt with the source of the throat-tightening, but then it would return again. Maybe it was the conditioning of being a woman in a culture and religion that silenced me. Maybe it was shame or low self-esteem. Maybe it was generational—

a symbolic and instinctual closing evolved from my Mennonite lineage. (Historically, Mennonites have often been known as "the quiet in the land.")

I had examined all of this, and yet . . . this throat-tightening persisted and nothing I did seemed to release its grip. It was limiting me at a time when I most wanted my voice to ring clear and true.

"Tell me, have you ever experienced a particular trauma that involved your throat?" my therapist asked. "Where you weren't able to breathe or talk?"

Whoosh—I could feel the truth of that landing as my brain finally caught up with my body.

"I can't believe I've never thought of this before," I said, my hand involuntarily rising to my throat. "It's my rapist's hands at my neck. He tried to choke me to death when I didn't give him what he wanted." Sharp intake of breath. "I am still living with my rapist's hands at my throat."

SOMETIMES I forget just how innocent I was. I mean that in more ways than one.

I was twenty-two years old. My roommate had just moved out, and I was planning to spend the summer alone before moving with my sister to another apartment in Winnipeg. I lived in a basement apartment on Wolseley Avenue, along the river, in a neighbourhood well loved by the granola crunchers (the eighties version of hippies) of the city. I was an aspiring granola cruncher, riding my bike to work every day and going to art shows, poetry readings, and protest marches on the weekends. I believed myself to be very grown-up and cultured, though I'd left the farm (and high school) only four years earlier and had spent the first two of those years in the cloistered embrace of a Bible college. (It might be worth mentioning here that I'd never had sex—not even close. Long before the term "purity culture" became a thing, I'd been steeped in a culture of shame around keeping my body pure.)

It was hot that summer. It was especially hot in that small basement apartment where the hot-water pipes for the whole building hung from the ceiling. (My former roommate had painted them pastel shades of pink and green to make them more palatable, but that didn't diminish the heat.) I kept the windows open at night and slept mostly naked.

Too many people since then have asked about those open windows, as though it were my own carelessness that allowed this to happen. They don't understand the oppressive heat. Or the victim-blaming things you shouldn't ask a rape survivor.

Just before my roommate moved out, I noticed some small holes cut into the curtains of our bedroom window. When I asked her about them, she swore she hadn't accidentally cut holes in the curtain, and then we both laughed it off as weird but irrelevant.

There are fragments from the night of the rape that hover slightly out of my memory's grasp. Other fragments are burned into my brain like a branding iron.

I remember the moment I woke up and a man was standing at the foot of my bed. As my eyes adjusted and my mind tried to make sense of what was happening, I saw that he wielded a pair of scissors. I recognized them as my scissors, and so I knew that, before I'd woken up, he'd had time to root through my things for a weapon. The other contents of the bag where he'd found the scissors were spread out on my former roommate's bed across the room, just behind him.

It still puzzles me that all of that happened—his climbing through the living room window, entering my room, and dumping out my bag and rooting through it—before I woke up. Not that anything would have turned out differently, but why didn't I wake up?

He swore he didn't want to hurt me, but he also stood there with his pants unzipped and his hand cupping his penis. Even before he came close to me, I could smell the unmistakable mixture of glue, rubbing alcohol, and body odour that suggested he was likely unhoused and also likely high.

What flashed through my mind as he stood there, before he touched me, was a story I'd read several years earlier on the back of a Sunday School handout for teenagers, about a girl who'd called out for God's help when threatened by a potential rapist. That man had been unable to reach through the invisible shield of her prayers to harm her. She'd walked away unscathed and with a testimony worthy of a Sunday School handout.

I started to pray out loud, begging God to protect me the way He'd protected that girl. I tried to picture the shield of protection, just the way I'd seen it illustrated in that Sunday School handout. Amazingly, when he heard my prayer, the man zipped up his pants and said, "Oh, are you a Christian? Me too!" And then he sat down on my bed, pulled a gospel tract from the pocket of his dirty pants, and started talking about his faith.

I'm not kidding. That really happened.

If this were a Sunday School handout, I'd be sure to end the story here with a tidy "God is so good to those who pray" message. But this isn't that story. We are no longer in Sunday School. My stories never wrap up that neatly.

At some point, he tired of his gospel tract, and got back to the reason he'd come.

The order of events has become blurry. Did I try to fight him off first and that's when he grabbed the scissors he'd dropped, held them menacingly over my head, and threatened to kill me? Or did he take off my underwear first and then, when I tried to fight him off, started choking me so hard I couldn't breathe and shoved my head between the bed and the wall as if to break my neck? Or did I fight him off after he stuck his finger in my vagina and then, after nearly being choked to death, decide that compliance was better than death? And when was it that he reached for my clitoris with his tongue? At what point did he try to insert his penis, but had trouble because it had gone flaccid and he couldn't revive his erection?

All those things happened during the two hours he was in my apartment—I just can't remember in which order. I do remember that sometimes he was calm and almost kind and wanted to curl up on the bed with me as though I were his childhood best friend and we were having a sleepover, and other times he was enraged and had death in his eyes. And I remember that sometimes I pleaded with him, sometimes I tried to cajole and even befriend him, and sometimes I fought for my life.

In the end, I convinced him to leave because the sun was coming up and I said that if I didn't show up for work, people would come looking for me. Because by then he seemed to think we were bonded in some twisted form of friendship, and I thought that if I played along with the charade, I might emerge alive. I promised that I would meet him under the bridge near my apartment the next night. (I believe the police went there at the appointed time but didn't find him.)

I may not remember all the details, but one thing was indelibly imprinted on my twenty-two-year-old body and is still present whenever my now fifty-seven-year-old body gets triggered. It is this: To stay alive and not have my head shoved between the bed and the wall, I need to soothe, coax, befriend, and give in to a man who is determined to take from my body whatever fills his needs. And if I don't give him what he came for, he will wrap his fingers around my throat and possibly kill me.

WHEN IS a trauma healed enough so that you don't carry the shadow of it with you into future relationships and choices? I have only found glimpses of the answer to that question in hindsight, and perhaps I don't have any answer at all.

A few days after the rape, I was determined to believe that I was fine and that life could return to normal. I insisted to my friends that I was fine, and even tried to stay on the relay team that I'd been training for to compete in a triathlon that weekend. My body gave out, though, and I quit the day before the race because my neck muscles were too sore for me to complete the forty kilometres on my bike. If I'd been honest with myself, I would have admitted that the greater limitation was the sheer terror that filled my body when anyone touched me or my mind returned to the scene of the crime.

A few years after the rape, I was still trying to convince everyone (including myself) that I was fine. I didn't know that I was carrying my rapist into my marriage with me, and that he would still clutch my throat years after my marriage ended. A trauma-informed therapist might have told me that I was still carrying my rapist with me, but at the time, I didn't think I needed a therapist.

Those fingers were at my throat the first time I knew it was my job to soothe my husband's anger and prop up his shaky self-esteem. Just as I sat on my bed with my rapist and tried to soothe him, I sat many times on the bed with my husband, trying to help him soothe his moods and learn to believe in himself more. (Isn't that just what a good wife does?)

Those fingers were there the many, many times in my marriage that I gave in to sex I didn't want to have. They were there when I cried myself to sleep at night because I didn't feel safe in my own bed but believed I needed to put my husband's needs above my own.

Those fingers were also at my throat each time I watched a woman being mistreated at work, every time a man got credit for something I'd done, and every time a man made a derogatory joke and I stayed silent. They were there on the soccer field when I watched coaches yell at my daughters and their teammates and I didn't say anything for fear of the consequences.

Those hands at my throat taught me how to stay silent, how to keep the peace, and how to appease those with power. They taught me to be kind to abusers while I guarded those being abused. They taught me that the only way to protect myself (and my children) was to put my body on the line and look after those who might harm us.

Recently, I read Sarah Polley's words in her book *Run Towards the Danger* (in an essay about her sexual assault at the hands of Jian Ghomeshi) and my breath caught in my throat.

> It can seem perplexing from the outside, this pull that many women experience to make things better for those who have hurt us. The impulse to smooth things over to keep ourselves safe, as well as the constant messages many of us have received in our lives to "make things nice" no matter what harm has been done, can be so deeply rooted that it often results in behaviour that can later appear nonsensical to an outside eye. (The betrayal of oneself that results from this "making things nice" with an attacker can also make one bleed on a subterranean level.)

Maybe it's built into us and maybe it's the result of generations of women before us who were taught throughout history to tend to abusers.

In a University of California study published in 2000, researchers revealed that typically studies of fight, flight, or freeze in times of stress focused on men and ignored women.

(A lot of research studies have done this since science was born.) "Although fight-or-flight may characterize the primary physiological responses to stress for both males and females, we propose that, behaviorally, females' responses are more marked by a pattern of 'tend-and-befriend.'" In tending, a person nurtures and protects with the intention of making it safe for people most at risk. In befriending, a person creates and maintains social networks that further support the safety of those at risk. Befriending can also involve what some have referred to as the "fawn" response to stress, where a person is overly solicitous toward the source of threat.

The first line of the study describes what my body knows whenever I feel those hands at my throat. "Survival depends on the ability to mount a successful response to threat." For me, as for many women before me, the instinct is not to fight or flee but to soothe and protect. Unfortunately, the last person I soothe or protect is generally myself.

WHILE AT university, a few years after the rape, I wrote and produced a play called *Woman Alone*, in which a woman has recently been raped by a man who climbed through her window. Throughout the play, she tries to move on with her life and her relationships, but no matter what she does, there is always a shadowy figure lurking at the edge of the scene. At one point, she has a tender moment with her boyfriend, but the shadowy figure moves toward her, and the moment is destroyed. The relationship doesn't survive because the rapist is still there.

I re-read that play this week and was amazed at how prescient it was, even though I didn't have the wisdom of foresight when I wrote it. In ways I've only become conscious of much later, that shadowy figure continued to lurk at the edges of my existence. Eventually, it took up residence in my body as a tightened grip on my throat.

Here are the final words from that play, typed out on my old Olivetti typewriter:

It will be nighttime soon, and I must try to sleep. Most nights I shut the window up tight and wrap my blankets around me. It gets very stuffy in here, but I can't open the window. Even during the day, it's hard to open it. I'd like to, sometimes—let the air into the room—but then I might get hurt again. Maybe tomorrow, I'll open the window... and the door... and you can come inside my room... and we can cry together... and then someday we'll learn to laugh. But not today. Today the window is closed. I don't know what will happen. Maybe I'll open it tomorrow... or maybe I'll nail it shut.

Recently, I discovered Tanya Tucker's song "No Man's Land," in which a girl named Molly Marlo is raped by a man named Barney Dawson after church one Sunday morning. After the rape, she shuts down and, though many men try to woo her, she turns them all down and soon develops a reputation as "no man's land." She becomes a nurse and one day she's called to the prison where Barney Dawson lies in pain, close to death. Molly Marlo denies him care, and he dies, his soul doomed to spend eternity wandering in no man's land.

I have wondered, sometimes, in my darker moments, what would happen if I met the man who raped me and was handed an opportunity like Molly Marlo's. Would I choose to save his life or let him go?

NOW, MORE than thirty years later, when a therapist helps me see that those hands are still at my throat, what comes next? Is there some miraculous healing I haven't found yet, in all my searching, that will loosen the grip once and for all?

Maybe. I haven't stopped searching. But it seems more likely that I will simply learn to live with this knowing, accepting that my body holds an emotional scar that will always be at least a little tender when it is bumped.

Perhaps it will be like a former therapist told me when my marriage ended and I sought help in resolving my fear of sexual and emotional intimacy. "It might be best to accept that there will always be some limitations for you and some situations where you may never feel safe," she said. "But that doesn't mean you can't find ways to work around the trauma wound. Perhaps you will never feel safe in sexual intimacy with men... but what about women? What's to stop you from exploring new forms of intimacy that don't have the same triggers for you?"

She may be right. I have discovered that my life can be quite fulfilling and joyful even if that trauma scar never entirely goes away. I have discovered that I can be sexually intimate with a woman and feel safer than I ever did with a man. If I never have sexual intimacy with a man again, do I risk becoming no man's land? Does that matter?

But maybe it's not as black and white as Molly Marlo's story would suggest. Maybe wholeness and healing are not synonymous. Maybe healing is more about gentle victories and tender, self-compassionate detours around the pain than it is about finding a triumphant, permanent fix that will return me to the version of wholeness I once thought I knew.

A STORY that's been seasoned by thirty-three years of living can, like a block of aged cheddar, take on a new flavour as it ages. In this particular story are pieces I mostly ignored in the first two decades of living with it, when my healing was the priority, but they have begun to feel relevant now. Perhaps, not unlike Molly Marlo, I want a chance to revisit the story that helped shape me and I want to write a new ending. Can I choose differently from Molly and wish for healing for my rapist, just as I heal myself?

I have become more practiced, in recent years, at seeing not only the personal aspect of a story like this, but the systemic aspects. It is not just a story of my own trauma—it is the story of trauma being passed from body to body to body. It is also the story of power, dominance, control, patriarchy, and even colonization. It's the story of how bodies are dominated and disenfranchised, how trauma becomes not just personal but systemic, and how harm and lateral violence disempower those at the edges.

To start with, it's the story of a man in a patriarchal world who took control over a woman's body as though he were entitled to it. It's the story of a young woman whose power was taken away from her, who did her best to soothe a man who had more—just as women have been taught to do throughout history. It's rape culture taken to its most ugly extreme.

But there's another layer. The man who raped me was not white. He was likely Indigenous. So this is also the story of a marginalized person who experienced his own challenges, and likely trauma. If he was Indigenous, this is also the story of a disenfranchised man, on land that was taken from his ancestors, who climbed into the apartment of a young woman whose family was given some of that land. It's a story within a larger story, of harm flowing in both directions, trauma passing from one lineage to another and back again, from colonizer to colonized and back again.

In other words, it's complicated, as all stories involving trauma are. There are threads in this story that weave back through history, back to the days when men first dominated women, back to the days when European settlers first colonized Canada. What was set in motion hundreds of years ago, on both sides of an ocean, landed in my young body the moment he laid his hands on me. And before that, it landed in him.

It is not by accident that I use the word "landed," because this story, zoomed out, is the same story as the land on which I live. My body is a landscape. Both raped and plundered, both suffering under colonization, patriarchy, and capitalism—systems that reduce bodies and land to resources, extracting what they need and throwing away the rest.

Now, more than thirty years later, I ask myself, "Is the trauma landing in my body part of this ancient narrative, and can my healing become part of it, too? Can I change this trajectory and pass on something different to the generations that come after me, and after him as well? Can I rise above these systems of harm and help to create something different?"

Like a virus, trauma passes from one body to the next, and so on, and so on. Until enough bodies have healed and developed the antibody that resists that virus, the spread continues, especially if the conditions are right for its spread. How, then, do we develop antibodies that resist the virus, and how do we change the conditions to stop the spread?

One thing I know for certain is that I want to choose differently than Molly Marlo. I want to choose healing not just for myself, but for my rapist, and for people in both his lineage and mine. I want my body and the bodies that come after mine to have the capacity to resist and transform not only the trauma itself, but the systems that continue to perpetuate the conditions for it to spread.

A few years ago, I participated in a sharing circle where settlers and Indigenous people gathered to talk about the harm done by colonization. After hearing the painful stories of what Indigenous families have suffered (and continue to suffer) across the country, I wrestled with whether my story had any place in the conversation. Finally, I spoke.

"I don't want to be part of the cycle of harm done in this country," I said, after sharing a small part of my story. "I want to work with you to transmit healing instead of pain, and I want to help change the systems that created the pain."

I haven't yet found a similar sharing circle where we can unravel and transmute the harm done by patriarchy, but if I were to find such a space, I would share similar words.

Recently, while working on this chapter and continuing to heal the story it contains, I went to sit at The Forks, where the Red River and Assiniboine River meet, where Europeans first settled on this land now called Manitoba. At that historic meeting place, where Indigenous people first welcomed those who would soon disenfranchise them, I sat quietly with the ancestors, imagining their stories, imagining what they all carried in their bodies and what they would pass on to their children and their children's children. Like an epidemiologist, I traced the trauma my body had been infected with back to its origin point. While the land held space for me, I held space for all the bodies infected between that time and now.

It was springtime as I sat by the river, and the trees along the riverbank were spilling their seeds onto the ground, planting their hope in the soil for the generations to come after them. Season after season, this land regenerates itself, transforming death into compost for new growth, transforming harm into possibility for the future.

I want to be like those trees, I decided, planting hope in the soil for generations to come. I want to pass on my healing, as the Haudenosaunee have taught us, to the seven generations that are to come.

IN A RECENT therapy session, something new showed up. Once again, I talked about the constriction at my throat, but this time I shared how it not only shows up when I'm anxious, but also when I am experiencing pleasure. "It's like there's something in my body that is afraid to trust in the pleasure and so it brings me back to memories of pain to keep me alert to the bad things that can happen to me."

"What do you feel in your body right now?" my therapist asked, as I rose to my feet.

"I feel spaciousness in the front part of my body, but there's still constriction in the back of my body and it's creeping back into my throat," I said. "It's like there's this shadowy figure moving in and trying to destroy the spaciousness and joy—like a childhood monster coming out from under a bed."

"Perhaps you can retrain your body," he said, "to hold both the spaciousness and constriction at once. Perhaps there's a way to live with the monster but to keep him from taking control." Then he invited me to say to myself: "I feel the tightening at my throat *and* I know that I am safe."

I stood there, holding a wide-open stance, saying his words out loud to my body, breathing in and out and in and out. With my eyes still closed, I began to rock with the breath, as though I were standing in waves, sometimes unstable and sometimes with my feet firmly grounded. My body had become like a shoreline, part of me solid like land and part of me fluid like water. I was liminal, unfinished and imperfect, sometimes grounded and sometimes wobbly. The waves, though they could unsettle me and make me feel anxious, could also soothe my tightened throat. Both things could be true in one body.

Gradually, holding both the spaciousness and the constriction, my body relaxed and I started to cry.

I WONDER, sometimes, why I never tell this story as a triumphant narrative; why I am always the scared and scarred victim, even more than thirty years later. What about the courage of that twenty-two-year-old who was clever enough to figure out how to survive? What about the ways she adapted to the changing moods she encountered, sometimes fighting for her life against the monster and sometimes gently soothing the wounded little boy inside the monster? And what about the many ways she carried that adaptability and will to live into her future?

Perhaps, all these years later, the constriction is not the rapist's hands at my throat, and to believe so is to give him too much of the storyline. Perhaps it is a benevolent force, a strength within me that knows how to adjust to each moment to survive. It may be maladaptive, as trauma imprints usually are, but it is not evil. It is simply my body telling my brain to "tend-and-befriend."

I am reminded of the Rilke quote I once had hanging on the wall above my desk. "Perhaps all the dragons in our lives are princesses who are only waiting to see us act, just once, with beauty and courage. Perhaps everything that frightens us is, in its deepest essence, something helpless that wants our love." It leaves me wondering how I can love those hands at my throat that have done their best to protect me.

LET ME try again with what is at the heart of this story, but let me tell it another way: I once knew a girl who was fierce, brave, and tender. Even though the world was a cruel place sometimes and people hurt her, she found the courage and strength to survive again and again. Her body kept doing its absolute best, in the only way it knew how, to protect her from harm, and she gradually learned to love that body more fully.

Not only did that girl survive and learn to heal, but she kept rewriting her stories until she found enough space in them for all the wounded to be held.

REFLECTION QUESTIONS

THIS STORY IS about a sexual assault that I suffered in my twenties. If you have a similar story, I hope that you can hold space for yourself in a tender way as you reflect on it (and find others to hold space for you). If you don't have a similar story, perhaps you have another that you can reflect on, of a time when the course of your life was altered in a way that was beyond your control.

1   How did this chapter impact you? What did this story bring up from your own stories?

2   My body still holds the memory of my rapist's hands, even though I didn't have conscious awareness of that for a long time. In what ways might your body be sending you messages about earlier parts of your life that still need attention and healing?

3   When my rape happened, some people implied that my carelessness in leaving the window open meant that the assault could have been avoided if I'd been more responsible. Victim blaming is common, especially when people feel uncomfortable holding space for another person's pain. In what ways can you relate to this in your own life? What can you do to release whatever shame that has left you with?

4   My therapist has helped me find practices that allow me to hold space for the trauma that still lives in my body. What practices might help you do the same for whatever resides in your body?

5   A narrative like this one is complex because of the layers of privilege, power, and trauma that exist in both of the key players in the story. In what ways does this resonate (or not) with your own stories?

6   My wish is for healing to extend beyond myself to include "all the wounded." You might not be ready for such a sentiment, and that's okay. Start with yourself. What healing do you need? If you're ready for it, what healing do you wish for other people?

7   In narrative therapy, people learn to retell their stories in ways that empower them. What story, or stories, might you need to find new ways to tell?

3

Faith and Flotation

FIRST DISCOVERED my love of floating when my children were small and we'd spend time at the beach. Exhausted from being the anchor at the centre of three small worlds, I would leave the children with their dad or other family members and wade in until the water was deeper than they were tall. Then I'd lean back and surrender myself to the water. Floating on my back, my ears beneath the surface, all sounds of demanding children were muffled and I could be liminal for a moment. In the world, but not of it; connected, but set apart. I loved the sound of that muted stillness. I still do, years later, though I no longer have as much need to drift away from the reach of my children or drown out the sounds from the shore.

For years now, my faith has floated in a similar liminal space. While I've waded into the water and become physically separated from the church I was once tethered to, I can still hear the muffled sounds that come from the shore. Sometimes that's exactly where I want to be and I feel free, and sometimes I wish I heard fewer of the voices still clamouring for my attention, still reminding me of the duties and expectations attached to the faith.

TO LIVE a Mennonite childhood is to learn to live at the edges, in the space in between. Not being as conservative or cloistered as some Mennonite groups, my family and church community were in the world, but not of it. We didn't live in a colony, nor were we surrounded by Mennonite neighbours, but we also didn't spend much time in the places where our non-Mennonite neighbours built community. We attended public school, but we didn't attend community bingo nights, dances, or any other events that might involve alcohol, dancing, or gambling.

A Mennonite in Canada grows up within a collectivist subculture under the shadow of an individualist over-culture. Community and individualism play tug-of-war with your identity. The result is a kind of cultural split personality. While clustering in groups and often keeping apart from the mainstream culture, Mennonites also tend to cling to their own people and (in sometimes covert and sometimes overt ways) shun former members who deviate from the faith.

There are good historic explanations for that aspect of our culture. Mennonites have a long history of setting themselves apart with beliefs and practices that are not part of the mainstream, plus the apartness was often forced on our ancestors when they were being discriminated against, tortured, and killed for those beliefs. Survival meant clinging to their own people and gathering in tight groups around shared beliefs and values. My people suffered at the hands of those in authority— first in Europe in the 1500s and 1600s, when they argued in favour of adult baptism and against the control of both Catholic and Protestant churches; and then in Russia in the 1800s and 1900s, when they stood for their belief in pacifism and against government intervention.

Strength, courage, and a commitment to justice thread through the Mennonite culture and belief system, but there is also a great deal of unresolved trauma and guardedness passed from generation to generation. This can result in a trauma bond between a person and their faith community, which makes it difficult to raise a dissenting voice (especially for a woman), leave on your own terms, or point out any abuse. In a trauma bond, as in abusive relationships and totalitarian systems, a disorganized attachment is formed: the source of comfort is also the source of greatest threat, which leaves a vulnerable person confused and destabilized (with their nervous system activated), longing for love but fearing the punishment attached to that love.

As a child, I felt tightly held and protected by my Mennonite community, but subconsciously, I always knew I risked losing that protection (plus the hope of an eternity in heaven) if I didn't live according to the church's rules. That left me with a dilemma, because living safely within the church's culture made me an outsider in the broader culture I longed to be a part of. When my classmates talked about their favourite TV shows, I couldn't contribute anything because we didn't have a TV. When they went to community dances, fairs, or bingo nights (which were important in the social fabric of our small town), I had no shared experience on which to build relationships. The language and context of belonging always eluded me (a challenge I carried into my adulthood).

To be safe in the church meant to be unsafe in the world. To be safe in the world meant to be unsafe in the church. There didn't seem to be any way to have both.

IN 2009, in a cloistered conservative Mennonite community in Bolivia, where people are allowed neither cars nor cellphones, a group of nine men were rounded up and later convicted of the rape and sexual assault of 151 women and girls in their own community, ranging in age from three to sixty-five years old. For years, these men had drugged families during the night by piping a narcotic spray (normally used to tranquilize livestock) into their homes. While everyone was unconscious, they entered the homes and raped the women and children.

For quite some time, women in the community had tried to convince male leaders that something was horribly wrong. They would wake up in the morning without clear memories of what had happened during the night but with signs in their beds and on their bodies that someone else had been there and something had happened to them. The men in the community dismissed their concerns as nothing more than female histrionics. Some of the women were accused of making up stories to hide illicit affairs.

Finally, the number of women coming forward was large enough that outside authorities were brought in, the situation was investigated, and the men were arrested and eventually convicted.

After the story became public, other more progressive Mennonite groups from the United States and Canada offered to send in counsellors who spoke Low German (the dialect of the community and many Mennonites around the world) to support the women, but the bishop of the colony rejected help on the victims' behalf. He was quoted in the press saying, "Why would they need counselling if they weren't even awake when it happened?"

Not long after the men were in prison, other Mennonite men began to lobby for the rapists to be released into the care of the community. Some were convinced that the men had been wrongfully convicted, and others believed that their Christian faith meant they should forgive and support those who caused harm. One Mennonite farmer in the community was quoted in a BBC article saying, "Our ministers always say we have to forgive, even if someone's committed a crime; that's why they've sent people to find out if the men can be freed."

Women were largely ignored, and some were even threatened for speaking against the men's wishes to bring the convicted men back to the community. Victims were told to put the past behind them and not disrupt the community with unnecessary conflict.

When pacifism and forgiveness are layered on top of a patriarchal culture, male rapists can be prioritized over female victims. It becomes more important to keep the peace and forgive (especially when those you've been asked to forgive are men) than it is to care for people who've been harmed (especially when the people harmed are women).

I wasn't raised in a culture quite as restrictive or patriarchal as that one, but I can see the same patterns played out in a subtler way in my own Mennonite upbringing. Though my dad was protective and supportive of me when I was raped, he was tortured by his desire to harm rather than forgive the man who did it to me. I have little doubt that, when he disappeared into the barn the day he learned of the rape, he begged God for a heart of forgiveness. He likely didn't know that it was his anger that made me feel loved, not his forgiveness.

Beliefs about forgiveness and pacifism can cause an internal war with our desire for justice and safety. Like the women in Bolivia, women in my lineage knew that it was risky to raise concerns that were disruptive, especially if it meant we'd make men feel uncomfortable. Our metaphorical Velcro dresses are heavy with the ways in which we've been taught that silence is the safest choice, so we often say nothing. When I read the story of the Bolivian rapes, my body ached with a shared knowing of what it's like to feel unprotected by those who believe the road to God is paved with forgiveness—and hopeless that anything can be done to change it.

In a 2011 study for her master's thesis, Elizabeth Krahn researched the impact of trauma on Mennonite women who fled Stalinist Russia during the Second World War and migrated to Canada. Though they'd lived most of their adult lives with stoic resilience, raising children and serving their households and churches the way good Mennonite women do, unresolved grief, depression, night terrors, anxiety, and paranoia surfaced later in life for many of these women. When Krahn dug into their stories, she learned that many had been raped and tortured and had watched family members be murdered when the Stalinist regime targeted Mennonite communities.

When some of those women (or their mothers and sisters) were raped by the soldiers, their pacifist husbands and fathers made no effort to protect them. So strong was their belief that they should not lift a hand in violence that they failed to defend the women they loved.

There's a multi-layered assault when you're victimized by one man and betrayed by another man who you hope would at least try to protect you. A truly embodied feeling of safety is hard to come by when those are the circumstances your nervous system is used to anticipating and protecting itself against.

My own Mennonite lineage, on both sides of the family tree, left Russia for Canada in the 1870s, when their right to conscientious objector status was being taken away and the government was trying to force them into army service. The Canadian government offered them land (subsequently displacing the

Anishinaabe residents of that land onto reserves) and promised to let them live with religious freedom. That was before Mennonites were being murdered and tortured by soldiers in Russia (as the women in the study experienced decades later), so that particular trauma is not part of my direct lineage, as far as I know. It's definitely in my cultural lineage, though, passed down through the bodies of the women who came before me. If my family had still been there, the women would have suffered the same fate, and they have always known that in their bodies. That's why my body registered so much surprise when my dad said he felt murderous toward my rapist—it just wasn't something we were used to hearing in our pacifist culture.

Not long after my separation, when I was grappling with the harm that had been done to me in my marriage, my brothers extended kindness to my former husband, even inviting him to join us on a family vacation to Florida. They didn't ask me how I'd feel about it; they were simply doing what their Christian beliefs taught them to do. My rational mind knows their hearts were in the right place (my brothers are both kind and supportive people), and I hold no ill will toward them. To be fair, I had told them little of the reality of my marriage, so they couldn't know what safety meant for me at that vulnerable time in my life, but their continued contact with my ex-husband still left my traumatized body with the sense that I, like my female lineage before me, couldn't count on support and protection when I needed it most. As with my dad after I'd been raped, I wanted my brothers' anger more than their forgiveness, but that's not the way they'd been conditioned to respond.

I LEFT the Mennonite faith and culture gradually, but I could still hear the voices from the shore no matter how far away I floated. The first outward break came in my early twenties, a few years after I attended a Mennonite Bible college in Stein-bach, the largely Mennonite town where I was born (before my family moved to a less Mennonite part of the province to help support a small church). Internally though, the breaking away started years before that. One of my most troubling moments in Bible college was the required course in evangelism, where one of the assignments was to witness about our faith (with the goal of conversion) to at least two people and then write a report about each experience. I hated the assignment but was so intent on pleasing those in authority that I would do what I hated in order to get good grades and be found worthy. Gritting my teeth, I wrote a letter in which I witnessed to my best friend from high school, and then had a very uncomfortable episode with a stranger in a mall down the street from the college. That might have been the moment I first admitted to myself that I was uncomfortable with this faith that expected me to con-vert people to ensure my salvation and graduation from college. (Incidentally, I have never heard from that friend since, and I still regret what I sent her.)

A few years later, a small group of friends I was part of broke away from the Mennonite church we all attended, gathering instead in the home of one of the young couples in our group. Together, we tried to do church and community differently, with less authoritarianism, patriarchy, and shame and a little more freedom around things like drinking, dancing, and our relationships with our bodies. That only lasted until the couple who hosted our weekly house-church fell into marital discord and separated.

After that, I returned to a Mennonite church for a few years, still hoping to find the safety and belonging that a loving com-munity could offer. It was a new congregation that felt more progressive, but when I started dating a Catholic, I sensed judgment. Most Mennonites grow up believing Catholics aren't "real Christians" and are nearly as far from God as pagans.

One of the many paradoxes of the Mennonite faith tradition (and many other Christian traditions, especially those in the evangelical spectrum) is that you find yourself in a strange kind of cognitive dissonance, trying to balance both unworthiness and superiority. On the one hand, you're inherently bad, but on the other hand, you're better than other people. While you're told again and again that you were born into original sin and can only be saved by God's grace, you're also led to believe you're among the elite group of people who have figured out the special code (known as the sinner's prayer) that grants access to God's grace.

Only the righteous will inherit the kingdom of God, and those considered "righteous" are few and far between. Atheists and agnostics are clearly outside the kingdom and condemned to hell. Muslims, Hindus, and anyone who worships another god—also out. Catholics—out, because they haven't accepted Jesus as their personal saviour. United Church (the only other church in the tiny town I grew up in)—far too liberal, and it wasn't clear that they even believed in sin. Anglicans? Too close to Catholics. Pentecostals? Too charismatic—they wave their hands in ecstasy, which looks too much like dancing. Baptists? They're pretty close because at least they baptize adults.

It's not just those on the more liberal or less-churched end of the religious spectrum who have questionable faith. Those who are more conservative and overly churched do, too. Some are even *too* Mennonite, like Holdemans or Old Colony (similar to Hutterites and Amish). They focus too much on dogma and rules, so it's hard to know if they have any real faith.

In other words, it wasn't very acceptable for me to become "unequally yoked" to a Catholic, especially one who didn't attend church regularly. (It became even less acceptable, though, years later when I divorced him.)

We got married in a Catholic church. Even though I was determined to forge my own path, and dating a Catholic may have been at least partially about rebellion, I still wanted to garner favour with my Mennonite community and family, so we invited my parents' pastor to do part of the service. We tried to have it both ways—a Catholic priest and a Mennonite pastor conducted the ceremony, and when it came to the reception, there was no alcohol during the dinner (in case my Mennonite relatives wanted to leave after that), but there was a dance after dinner with alcohol available. (In retrospect, by trying to please everyone, we probably pleased no one.)

After we married, we sporadically attended a Catholic church, but when the babies started to come, I worried about raising them without a solid biblical foundation (with an underlying fear that I might be condemning them to hell), so I pushed for us to find a church that at least had a strong children's ministry. My sister attended a Christian Reformed church, and that felt like it was midway between Catholic and Mennonite, plus it had a strong focus on children's ministry, so we followed her there. My dad expressed his concern, asking whether that church would teach us about sin.

It was a good move for me and for my growing family at the time. That small community-oriented church provided me with what I'd been searching for—a place where love and acceptance were offered with little shame and few conditions. Though we were sporadic in our attendance at the beginning, we became more fully committed to it when church members surrounded us with love and support when our son, Matthew, was stillborn.

The three-week period leading up to (and including) the loss of Matthew was the most spiritually connected time of my life.

I was hospitalized halfway through the pregnancy, for a surgery meant to close a prematurely opened (or "incompetent") cervix. The surgery failed, though, and the membrane protecting the baby was ruptured, putting the pregnancy at risk. For weeks I waited and hoped my baby would be born alive. In the hospital, I often had a palpable sense that there was a spiritual presence in the room with me and I could communicate with that presence, especially during the nighttime when the hospital was quiet. Those mystical moments left me hungry for more of the same, so I dove back into my faith, hoping to find something more alive than I'd experienced before.

In 2004, I left my government job and accepted a position at an international development non-profit that represented almost all Christian denominations across Canada. Nearly everyone whose faith I'd once been taught to be suspicious of—Catholics, Pentecostals, United Church, and everything in between—worked together in their common goal to alleviate hunger in the world. The collaborative effort helped heal the part of me that had felt rejected when I'd married outside the faith and it helped expand my faith to include many other pathways to God.

I continued to wrestle, though, never entirely comfortable with the fundamentals of the faith. I spent a lot of time, for example, trying to understand the concept of worship. Why would God create people so that they could bow down and worship Him? Wasn't that the epitome of narcissism? I asked several people that question, including someone who'd made worship the core of his academic work, and received some answers that made it seem less narcissistic, but I was never fully satisfied (and I stopped asking because it seemed to offend people).

A year after starting my job at the non-profit, I took my first trip to Africa and visited several places in Kenya and Tanzania where our organization supported food-related projects. On that trip, more cracks formed in my faith when my eyes opened to the colonizing impact the Christian church has had in that part of the world. A Kenyan lay pastor travelled on the bus with us for part of the trip, and one Sunday morning our group (donors and staff of the non-profit) held a small church service in the pub of the hotel where we were staying. This young minister, who'd been trained by Western missionaries, preached a message straight out of the prosperity gospel. If you were faithful to God, he said, you'd get a good wife and a nice house and you wouldn't get AIDS. Looking around at our circle of relatively privileged white people from Canada—people who had all the things the minister wanted—this man had reason to believe that we must be closer to God. Somewhere, he'd picked up a belief (and attached it to his Velcro clothing) that he was worth less in God's eyes than relatively wealthy white people.

Another Kenyan man told me that many of the most corrupt government leaders in Africa had gone to missionary schools and had been influenced by the model of white missionary men who were authoritarian, patriarchal, sometimes abusive, and not accountable to anyone for their behaviour other than themselves and their version of God. It shook my perception of Africa and exposed some of the complexity at the root of the poverty and injustice that's present in many places.

I came home feeling disillusioned about the influence Christianity has had around the world, especially because of its enmeshment with colonization. The cracks only deepened when I heard more and more stories about the harm done by residential schools in Canada, many of which were run by churches, in partnership with the government.

Because the church I was attending was a relatively safe place at the time, when I gave a presentation about my trip, I shared honestly about my disillusionment. Some in the congregation were receptive while others weren't. Not long after that, I was nominated to become an elder in the church because someone thought my leadership capacity would be an asset in helping the congregation continue to evolve. I was fairly certain I wasn't the right person for the job, and not in the right place spiritually, but my friend Rob (who was the pastor at the time) convinced me that if I was disillusioned with the church, I should help to change it from the inside. After praying about it, I decided to take him up on the challenge. A few people who'd been bothered by my presentation let me know that they questioned the wisdom of my appointment, but I accepted it anyway.

About halfway through my three-year term as an elder, the elder board was pushed to take a stand against same-sex marriage. It had just become legal in Canada, and a few of the more conservative members of the congregation were afraid we might someday be expected to perform same-sex marriages in our church. At the time, I was still working out my own belief about same-sex marriage, examining which of the precepts of my childhood faith I wanted to hang on to and what I wanted to pluck off my Velcro dress. I didn't feel ready to take a firm public position on it but was suddenly pushed to. Trembling in my seat at an elder meeting, I said that if they chose to ban same-sex marriage, I would no longer be an elder in that church. I hadn't yet admitted to myself that I was bisexual, but knew I couldn't be part of a church that wasn't truly welcoming of my gay friends. The matter was dropped, and we ended up taking no stance on either side of the issue. (Incidentally, that particular congregation has since become more welcoming to same-sex relationships, though the denomination they're part of has not.)

I stayed on the elder board for the remainder of my term but didn't agree to a second term. I didn't feel committed enough to carry on, and I wasn't confident that I could create the kind of change that might help the church become a place I wanted to stay—a place where I felt truly safe and welcome.

ON EASTER WEEKEND 2011, I suddenly felt like I was about to lose the four pillars that had been the foundation of my life. The year before, I'd walked away from a successful career at the non-profit to start my own business, and I was now financially wobbly. My family found out that weekend that my mom had cancer that would likely kill her. I finally admitted to myself that I wanted out of my marriage and told my husband (on the same day we found out Mom had cancer) that I would only keep trying if he found a marriage counsellor who could help us. Then, as I sat in church on Easter Sunday morning, I realized that the Easter story no longer held any meaning for me.

The irony of everything seemingly dying on a weekend that's centred on Christ's death and resurrection is not lost on me.

Career, parentage, marriage, and church—what could be more foundational than those four pillars? It took another four years, partly because I was too overwhelmed and scared to let go of my marriage and church while my mom was dying, but eventually all four were gone. Mom died in 2012, and I left the church and the marriage in 2015. When I walked away from my marriage, it also made sense to walk away from the church— both institutions had started to feel like they were binding me in a life mapped by other people's expectations, wishes, and rules and I needed to find my own way.

I was reluctant to throw away my faith completely, though, so I again looked for a church that felt more like home. I made only a half-hearted effort to find such a place and soon realized I didn't feel the need to leave my house on Sunday mornings. The outdoors became my church, as did the laughter of my children and the love of my friends. Worship started to make more sense when I simply stood in awe of a sunset.

ASK ANYONE raised to believe in hell and they will tell you stories of their fear of being "left behind" (even those of us raised before the popular book and film series of that name existed). I remember numerous occasions when I'd come home from visiting a friend or I'd come in from the barn after doing my chores to find nobody in the house, and the panic would rise as I considered that the rapture might have happened, and I was not among the righteous. That kind of fear, established in childhood before the brain and body are fully developed, takes a long time to leave a person, even years after you stop believing in hell.

After I left the church, I still heard voices from the shore, voices that told me I was sinful and being left behind. While outwardly I was putting my life back together after getting divorced and leaving the church, and my business was beginning to flourish, inwardly, I still struggled with shame, self-doubt, fear, and an ongoing anxiety that I would be rejected by my family and community if I admitted that I no longer saw the church as necessary for me. I avoided conversations about faith and was easily triggered if I sensed a family member judging me for not going to church or for getting divorced. On that trip to Florida with my siblings and our children (which my ex-husband did not attend, by the way), I sat through an uncomfortable church service on Christmas morning because I didn't want them to know how little faith I had left. I still wanted to be part of the fold. I still longed for the safety and belonging I thought I could only get from the church and my family. Appearing to share the same religious beliefs was the only way I knew how to be seen as acceptable within my family of origin.

When I discovered Marlene Winell's work on religious trauma syndrome, I felt seen in a way that I hadn't felt in a long time. In her book, *Leaving the Fold*, Winell talks about how those raised with evangelical and/or fundamentalist beliefs often struggle for years, long after they've left the church. Symptoms of religious trauma syndrome include impeded development (social, emotional, sexual, et cetera); depression, anxiety, or other mental health concerns; poor decision-making skills; lack of self-confidence and self-esteem; a sense of isolation; pervasive feelings of guilt and shame; and difficulty forming healthy adult relationships. I saw all of those symptoms in myself.

Winell writes, "A rigid religion fosters dependency on the external authorities of 'God' (as defined by the religion), scripture, and the church leaders for guidance in truth. Ultimately, a rigid religion erodes the natural contentment and confidence with which every child begins life and which every healthy human being needs."

Even now, after years of working through this, I still feel anxiety rise in my body when I think about sharing this piece of writing with family members. Will I be abandoned? Will I go to hell? Thankfully, a good therapist and some very good friends have helped me find my way toward greater self-love and self-trust, and I know that, even though I still get triggered occasionally, I'll be okay in the end. I just keep working at it.

WHILE I was deconstructing my faith and healing the trauma left behind in my body, I found that beneath the resistance to the indoctrination there remained some desire to reconnect with my roots and reclaim the parts that still had value. It's an honourable thing to be part of a lineage of non-violence, peace-seeking, community building, and conscientious objection, and those are all building blocks that have contributed to how I live and offer service in the world. I want to see the light while not being afraid to peer into the shadows.

A few years ago, I started making regular pilgrimages to the place, less than an hour from my house, where the Rat River meets the Red River. There, in 1874, my ancestors arrived from Russia, climbed off a boat, and began to build farming settlements on land allotments they'd been given by the government (which, incidentally, the government referred to as "reserves," perhaps indicative of the way the government viewed these new immigrants and their peculiar faith). I wanted to connect with the courage of those ancestors who'd left a country that no longer kept them safe, to build a new life that offered more safety for their children. Sitting at the intersection of the two rivers, I thanked them for choosing peace, for fighting to survive, and for passing their courage down to me.

Then, before travelling to the Netherlands for some teaching work, I dug far enough back into my family tree to find the places in Europe, mostly in the Netherlands and Germany, where my people had originated, back in the fourteenth, fifteenth, and sixteenth centuries. I wanted to connect with those who'd been brave enough to stand against oppressive authority, even at the risk of losing their lives. While in the Netherlands, I rented a car and spent time in several towns where my ancestors had lived and where some had been executed. I thanked them for standing up for peace and justice and for passing on their courage and resilience.

On my bookshelf, near where I currently sit, is my dad's copy of *Martyrs Mirror: The Story of Seventeen Centuries of Christian Martyrdom, from the Time of Christ to A.D. 1660.* (The even longer title is *The Bloody Theatre, or Martyrs Mirror of the Defenseless Christians, Who Baptized Only upon*

Confession of Faith, and Who Suffered and Died for the Testimony of Jesus, Their Saviour, from the Time of Christ to the Year A.D. 1660.) Second only to the Bible, this is considered a most precious book in Mennonite households. It's 1,157 pages long and includes stories, songs, letters, and prayers of "defenseless Christians" who were killed for their faith. It was compiled and published in 1659 by a Dutch Mennonite, Thieleman J. van Braght, to strengthen the faith of his fellow believers, and translated into German in 1748 at the time of the French and Indian War for the same reason. In 1886, just after my ancestors landed at the Rat River, the text was translated into English to challenge generations of Christians in North America.

Once, when I was a young teenager, our family arrived at our tiny rural church for a special evening service to find a sign on the door. "It is illegal to gather here," was the essence of the message. "Those who worship here will be tried for heresy and sentenced to death."

A church member greeted us at the door and whispered something to us about a secret meeting place in the basement of a nearby church member's home. With a little excitement and perhaps a little fear, we made our way to the alternative meeting space.

This re-enactment of the early days of our Mennonite ancestors in Europe was meant to give us a sense of what it was like when they were tortured and killed for their beliefs and their defiance against the powerbrokers in both church and state. Just like *Martyrs Mirror*, it was meant to strengthen our faith so that we'd be prepared for persecution.

While I have been skeptical of the attachment to (and glorification of) martyrdom and victimhood among Mennonite Christians (which I think contributed to the response in

Manitoba to the COVID-19 pandemic, when many in predominantly Mennonite communities became convinced that the government was trying to harm them with vaccinations and social isolation mandates), I also wanted to explore what drove my ancestors to such extremes in defending what they believed in. Perhaps more than anything, I wanted to find a female ancestor whose strength, courage, and passion for justice for the oppressed I could claim as part of my lineage. (I may have romanticized that idea a little too much.)

There are several tales of women in *Martyrs Mirror*. There was the woman whose mouth was stuffed with gunpowder before she was tossed into the flames; the two sisters who were drowned together; and the woman who refused to recant even after screws were applied to her thumbs, fingers, and hips. And then there was the woman who was pregnant when first apprehended and who was allowed to go home until her baby was born. "She did not flee, but boldly remained," and when they came back for her, after the baby was born, she surrendered and was executed by the sword.

The story that impacted me most was of "a very God-fearing and pious woman" named Maeyken Wens, of the city of Antwerp, who was burned with a tongue screw in her mouth. Her fifteen-year-old son Adriaen "could not stay away from the place of execution on the day on which his dear mother was offered up; hence he took his youngest little brother, named Hans (or Jan) Mattheus Wens, who was about three years old, upon his arm and went and stood with him somewhere upon a bench, not far from the stakes erected, to behold his mother's death." When they brought her out, though, Adriaen lost consciousness and didn't wake up until his mother was dead. Afterward, he hunted through the ashes to find the screw that had kept her tongue fastened and he held on to it, in remembrance of her.

In prison before her execution, Maeyken was "subjected to much conflict and temptation by so-called spirituals (ecclesiastics), as well as by secular persons, to cause her to apostatize from her faith." *Martyrs Mirror* includes five letters written by Maeyken while she was in prison: two to her husband (a minister), two to the teenage son who later attended her execution, and one to another minister. In those letters I hoped to find clues about what she cared so passionately about and why she was in prison while her husband walked free, but I was disappointed. Instead, she talks about how she regrets not being more thankful to God in the midst of her adversity; how she doesn't want her husband to spend money coming to visit her or bringing her food; how her heart is "fixed to offer up a sacrifice to the Lord"; how she's a "poor miserable creature"; how often she failed at following her husband's Christian instruction; how weak she is and "such a poor writer"; how she implores her son to trust God instead of himself and to "hate everything that is loved by the world and your sensuality"; and how God will "chasten" her son when he does evil.

Instead of the courageous, liberated female ancestor I'd been seeking, I found in Maeyken a woman not unlike my own mother, full of shame and self-deprecation, living under the bounds of a patriarchal religion that made her fearful of hell, and believing that the way to find favour with her God was to make her body a sacrifice to Him. Her final letter to her son, Adriaen, written the day she received her death sentence, had a line that was much like a line in one of the letters I received from my mom in my early adulthood. "Write me a letter as to what your heart says," Maeyken writes, "whether you desire to fear the Lord; this I should like to know. But you must write it better than the last two letters were written." The very next day (perhaps even before he received the letter), this young man stood on a bench to watch his mother die and probably lived the rest of his life with the fear that he'd never live up to her expectation of him. I imagine the tongue screw he found in the ashes may have served as a daily reminder of the way he'd disappointed her.

I don't know whether Maeyken is in my direct lineage, but I can see the pattern of her trauma and her son's trauma passed down through the generations and landing in my relationship with my mom. Just as I continue to do my best to send my mom love and forgiveness, and to heal what was left behind so that my daughters don't inherit it, I reach back through the generations to send Maeyken and her son the same. May they all be at peace.

I STILL love to float, but now I often do it in sensory deprivation float tanks. In those, there is no sound from the shore and, though I am confined to a small tank, I feel surprisingly free. Sometimes the noise that used to come from the shore comes from inside my own head, but I am learning to soothe whatever voices sound more like old wounds and conditioning than my own true voice.

My friend Randy holds a PhD in Jungian studies and retired a few years ago from his career as a United Church minister. For the last fifteen or so years, Randy has offered me a glimpse into what a liberated faith, without all the baggage that I once carried, might look like. When I grew tired of a masculine-only version of God, Randy loaned me books from his library about the feminine divine. When I was trembling in front of the elder board, speaking out in support of same-sex marriage, Randy had already officiated at same-sex weddings. When I was in a period of deconstruction, I asked Randy how he understood these words of Jesus that are tightly held by evangelical and fundamentalist Christians: "I am the way and the truth and the life. No-one comes to the Father except through me." He offered an expanded definition of "the way," suggesting that Jesus never meant for it to be so narrowly focused that it turned Him into an ideology. "It's one of the most misused passages from the Bible," he said.

Almost everywhere I needed to go in the evolution of my faith, Randy had already been. He shone the light on my path without holding any attachment to whether or not I chose the same path as he had. (He would have failed my evangelism class at Bible college.) No matter what I chose to believe, I could always count on Randy's love.

Randy phoned me a few months before I wrote the original version of this chapter to tell me that he was diagnosed with ALS and was expecting to die in the not-too-distant future.* At the time of this writing, he'd already become confined to a wheelchair and his speech was beginning to slur. He'd signed the papers for medically assisted dying, and when he could no longer communicate and his care would become too much of a burden for his family, Randy planned to release himself from this life on his own terms.

Randy lived in Nova Scotia, so I couldn't visit him easily or take him out for any of the long drives in the countryside that were once a treasured part of our relationship. Instead, we committed to a conversation over Zoom every couple of weeks until the time came when communication would be impossible.

---

* Between writing this chapter and the publication of this book, Randy has died. While he was still alive, I recorded myself reading the last portion of this chapter on video and sent it to him so that he'd know the place he held in my life. Journeying with him in his last year on earth was one of the great privileges of my life, and I will continue to carry his spirit with me. Before he died, while he could still communicate clearly, he told me that he believed that death would be a release into "pure joy." I will always picture him that way—eternally joyful. And free.

Even as he was dying, Randy was teaching me about faith. Though he once lived a large and adventurous life, travelling all over the world, Randy was not bitter about the fact that he was now confined to the ground floor and would likely never again visit the kitchen of his own house, or his home office where all the mementos of his career and lifelong love of travel were on display. Because he was especially vulnerable in the middle of a pandemic, few people could visit him, and he couldn't see his grandchildren at Christmas. And yet, Randy was remarkably at peace, and my conversations with him were some of the most joyful and easy conversations that I have had with anyone. He told me he'd laughed more in the last six months, since his diagnosis, than he remembers laughing in his lifetime. He said that in his time in the ministry, he had met many people who were dying, and some were joyful and at peace while others were resistant and angry. He was choosing to end his days at peace, with his faith and his contemplative prayer practice helping him to find that peace.

When I asked about the source of his peace, Randy said that he believed his soul would live on after he was finished with his body, and so his death would simply be a change of address and way of being. He didn't use any of the language of heaven that I grew up with, and simply saw himself held in the embrace of a loving divine who never threatened to abandon him to hell for anything he did while on earth. There was no trauma bond in his faith. As a result, his final days did not hold any of the anguish that was part of my mom's experience when she feared that her children or grandchildren might never join her on the other side.

This unconditional love and untethered peace that I witnessed in Randy helped me heal and grow in the years after I left the church and my marriage. This spirit is now woven into my work offering people what I have always longed for—

a space where love, safety, and belonging are not dependent on their faith, identity, ideology, or adherence to a doctrine or a set of rules.

Today, my faith is not tethered to an ideology or a certain definition of God. I remain open to the version of the divine that Randy cherished, and I find there is comfort in believing that a higher power is available to me, one who holds me when I'm sad or lost and who will continue to hold me even after my body is buried in the ground. That version of God is not shrouded in guilt or shame or expectations. It doesn't demand of me martyrdom or self-flagellation and doesn't require that I convert anyone to a certain dogma. Instead, it offers liberation and love.

I now often refer to the divine as Mystery, because I no longer have a clear definition of what or who it is. I experience Mystery as the presence that I feel when I wander through the woods or along the shore and listen to birdsong. It's what I feel when I stand eye-to-eye with a deer and know that we are connected. It's what I knew to be present whenever I spent time with Randy or others whose love is not dependent on my righteousness. It's the sky, the tree, the eagle, and the sea. It's the feeling in my body when I hold myself with love.

It's the salt water beneath me in the float tank, lifting me up with tenderness as I lay there, naked, with nothing to hide and no voices making demands from the shore.

REFLECTION QUESTIONS

MANY OF OUR beliefs are inherited before we are conscious of what we are being taught. They're attached to our Velcro clothing by family members who found them valuable for their own lives or inherited them themselves and didn't know how to detach from them. These might be spiritual, political, or cultural beliefs, or beliefs about a family's place in the world. Sometimes a belief is subconscious and doesn't reveal itself until it has been challenged or until we see it mirrored in someone else's story (even in fictional books and movies).

1 What beliefs did you inherit from your lineage? How were you taught those beliefs?

2 How did those beliefs contribute to your feelings about yourself? How did they contribute to your sense of safety and belonging in the world? Which are meaningful for you and worth hanging on to?

3 Which parts of the belief systems that you inherited no longer serve you now and need to be deconstructed?

4 How does it feel to let go of beliefs that are still important to others in your lineage?

5 What have you lost? Or what are you afraid of losing?

6 How do you create the foundation of your life? What might support you in finding your inner core of strength?

7 I sought out a female member of my lineage who I could look up to (in *Martyrs Mirror*) and found only wholly human and

fallible people just like me. Who, if anyone, in your lineage do you consider to be a role model?

8   My friend Randy helped me find a more liberated faith. Whose path serves as an inspiration to you? (It might be someone you know or someone you've never met.)

4

The Woman Behind the Door

AT THE Weisman Art Museum in Minneapolis, there's a permanent installation by Nancy Reddin Kienholz and Edward Kienholz that was built to represent a fictional building called Pedicord Apts. After walking through an apartment lobby that's reminiscent of some of the old character buildings I lived in in my twenties (in other words, in need of renovations), you enter a hallway that becomes smaller and more claustrophobic as you move toward the exit sign at the far end (where there is no actual exit, just a window with clouded glass). None of the apartment doors in the hallway open, but if you lean toward a door, you can hear a snippet of life happening on the other side. At one door, a couple argues; at another, a family watches a game on TV.

When you lean against the last door, where the roof and walls are the narrowest, a woman is weeping—forever weeping.

You can step away and the motion sensor stops the sound, but when you lean in again (as I did many times), the woman is still weeping.

The first time I visited the gallery, I was haunted by this woman and could hardly pull myself away from the door. While my daughters explored other parts of the gallery, I stepped into the hallway several times and leaned quietly against the door to listen to the woman weep. I couldn't explain why I felt so drawn to her at the time, simply that I needed to hold vigil outside the door.

The first time I encountered the weeping woman was after I'd separated from my husband and before I'd filed for divorce. The next time I visited Minneapolis, the divorce had been newly finalized, and I'd become sole owner of the house we'd shared for seventeen of the twenty-two years of our marriage. I visited the gallery a second time for the singular purpose of spending more time with the weeping woman. This time my daughters weren't with me, so I could linger in the hallway longer.

Recently, I discovered that you can visit the hallway of the Pedicord Apts. on a virtual tour of the Weisman Art Museum. There is no sound, though, so the weeping woman can't be heard. I tried it once, clicking on the arrow until I arrived at her door, but it made me feel sad and a little desperate to move down the hallway on my computer screen and not be able to lean in and listen. I couldn't shake the feeling that I was betraying her and leaving her even more isolated than before.

The weeping woman and I are bonded because I know her— deep in my bones, I know her. Like her, I have cried many, many tears behind closed doors, desperately unhappy and yet, like her, frozen in time. For too many years, I could not emerge from behind that door because I didn't know how to explain my tears in a way that would make sense to anyone on the other side of the door.

I visit her because I don't want either of us to be so alone anymore. Maybe she doesn't know there's someone on the other side of the door who hears her—but I know, and that matters. If I could, I'd sneak in quietly and sit down on the wooden floor with her (because that's where I imagine her to be, as though her misery makes her unworthy of a comfortable chair). I wouldn't say a word. I'd just pass her tissues and tea.

THE LONELINESS and despair are hard to name when you're in the middle of it. When you're in a marriage that continually causes pain, both for you and your partner, it messes with your sense of what is true and what you're imagining, especially when you don't know how to articulate that pain and you wonder if you're taking it all too seriously. Because you chose this, you learn to pretend the pain is not there, and you convince yourself that you probably don't have any right to expect better.

"I should be happy, shouldn't I?" I kept trying to convince myself that I should. M was a good man; we had a good life together... didn't we? There were many things about him that other wives envied. He cooked and cleaned; he changed diapers and got up during the night with crying babies. He joined the parent committee at school, coached soccer, and signed up for enough parent volunteer roles to make up for my absence. He was funny and friendly. He made people laugh. He played well with children. He was an involved parent who gave me freedom to go on business trips when I needed to.

I was happy sometimes. It wasn't always horrible. And yet, again and again, I was that woman, crying behind my door.

I WAS THE woman behind the door every time I said yes when I wanted to say no. I was her whenever I changed my no to yes because I knew there would be consequences if I didn't give in to the repeated, often coercive, requests. I was her when my body was touched even though consent had been denied.

Our sex life was fraught with M's neediness and my guardedness. In retrospect, I see so clearly the trauma in both of our bodies—one seeking affirmation and love through sex, and one pulling back because of the invisible marks left behind by a rapist and a religion.

Far too many times, I gave in, even when my body screamed, "No!" The reasons are endless: I thought it was my duty as a good wife; I felt guilty for hurting him; I worried that something might be wrong with me for not wanting sex more often; I didn't believe I was worthy of more tenderness and respect; and I kept believing that, if only I kept trying, sex would become more pleasurable.

Most of all, though, I did it to keep the peace. Too many rejections would result in M's moodiness that affected everyone in the house. His impatience would intensify, and soon the arguments would start.

I knew the signs of the shifting mood and then I'd say yes the next time, assuming that's what I needed to do to keep the house peaceful. Afterward, I'd cry myself to sleep. Sometimes I'd even cry during sex—the loneliness of that unwilling yes aching to be expressed.

I WAS that woman behind the door when my former husband attempted suicide. And then, years later, when he attempted it again.

The first time it happened, I was halfway through the pregnancy with our first child. I'd been through a scare two months earlier, at the end of my first trimester, when I started to bleed profusely and spent two nights in the hospital. I didn't lose the baby, but the anxiety didn't entirely leave me after that.

Then came the emotional tailspin when M made a mistake at work and started having major panic attacks. Neither of us knew what to do.

I went into fixer mode and tried to get him help. I booked him a visit with a psychologist, and he came out of that appointment looking despondent. I checked him into an overnight mental health facility a few days later, and that, too, made little difference. He pleaded with me to bring him back home, and I did.

I tried both gentle love and tough love, first soothing and supporting him, and then pushing him to get over it. I made many mistakes in my desperation for the world to feel safe again, suddenly unsure of how stable the home was that I was bringing a child into.

One day I thought he was finally on the mend. He kissed me goodbye in the morning, put his hand on my belly, told me to take care of our baby, and left for work. I called his office from mine a couple of hours later, only to discover that he'd never arrived. I panicked and started calling people who might have seen or heard from him—his brother, cousins, and parents. Nobody had.

Late that evening, his brother called from the hospital. "He's here," he said. "He's alive, but he's hurt himself badly. They'll need to do surgery."

A week later, after addressing only his physical wounds and failing to transfer him to a psychiatric ward as they'd said they would, the hospital discharged him and entrusted him to my care instead. Again, I struggled to find the right help, driving him to support groups and booking him therapy appointments. My body stayed vigilant, never knowing what would send him into despair again. Many times, I cried behind closed doors.

Fifteen years later, it happened again. This time, we had three daughters, ages eight, thirteen, and fourteen. This time, instead of being pregnant with a baby, I was about to bring a business into the world—once again turning my attention away from him.

After years of waiting for the right time, I was on the verge of resigning from my job as director of communications at a non-profit to launch my long-dreamed-of business. For five years, my salary had supported the family while M attended university, and then for another two years, I'd stayed at that job while he tried to find full-time work. It had always been our plan that once his income could support the family, I would quit my job to start my business, but at his first promising job, a problem at work triggered panic attacks and things escalated quickly. I was in denial about it at first, trying to pretend this was just a momentary blip and he would be fine. I left town for a conference, determined to continue as though life were normal, but while I was there, he spiralled further. He dropped off our daughters at his sister's and checked himself into an overnight facility.

A few days after I returned home, M's mom called me at work. He'd driven to his parents' house in the country and, because he appeared lethargic and not himself, she'd pushed him until he'd confessed that he'd taken a lot of pills. Somehow, she got him into her car and drove to our house at the edge of the city where I met them and rushed him to the hospital. His mom stayed at our house and waited for our girls to come home from school. As I drove, I screamed at him to stay awake.

Once again, mental health care at the hospital was sub-par. This time, they checked him into the psychiatric ward after a few days in the emergency room, but then they paid little attention to him beyond taking his belt and shoelaces away. The only mental health care he got was a fifteen-minute visit from a different psychiatrist each day. Once again, I tried to find the right help, even going so far as to sneak him out of the psych ward (against the wishes of the psychiatrist) to take him to see a psychologist I'd found through the help of a friend. Once again, I made many mistakes, feeling panicky about when I'd have to bring him home to our children.

Early in M's hospital stay, before he was in the psychiatric ward, when I remarked to the third psychiatrist to visit the bedside that he was the only one who'd bothered to introduce himself to me, that psychiatrist opened up to me about how disheartening it was to work in such a broken system, where he could only drop in on a patient for fifteen minutes instead of providing meaningful support. "I quit this job every single day," he said. "And yet I'm still here." I wanted to tell him, "I quit this marriage every single day. And yet I'm still here."

The closed door I cried behind this time was my van door as I drove from home to school to the psych ward, and then from the psych ward to the soccer field, managing M's care while keeping our daughters' lives as close to normal as possible. I was exhausted and scared, but the emotion that surprised me the most this time was anger. It burned in me like a fire about to lose control. My need to keep everyone safe eclipsed my anger, though, so I stuffed it down.

PERHAPS IT'S human to be able to recognize the patterns of another person's behaviour before we can recognize the patterns in our own. And perhaps I was trying too hard to place the burden of responsibility for my pain on his shoulders, rather than see the ways that I was contributing to the brokenness in our marriage. About a year after his second suicide attempt, I insisted on marriage counselling, hoping it would bring to light what I couldn't see. Before the end of our first session together, the therapist said that she wanted to see M separately. He attended a few sessions, and then we went back to see her together. This time I asked whether I could have some separate sessions, too, certain the problems were not only his responsibility. When I was alone with the therapist, I asked her to help me understand my contribution to the dysfunctional parts in our marriage. I don't remember exactly what she said, but what I picked up from her was that she largely held him responsible and thought I was foolish to stay. The session ended fifteen minutes early, and I left feeling frustrated, with no better understanding than I'd had before.

We tried another therapist a year or two later, but I didn't get any closer to understanding myself in the context of the relationship. A year after that, still confused by it but no longer willing to abandon myself in my efforts to keep the marriage together, I asked M to move out. It was the hardest thing I've ever done. I so badly wanted a different outcome.

SOMETIMES, EVEN a few years after my marriage ended, I was still that woman crying behind the door. Text messages would come from M, and I would suddenly become the woman I'd been for twenty-two years, always hypersensitive to his moods, responsive to his needs, and vigilant to what would impact my children. I could feel my body fire into alertness when his name appeared on my phone, and though my rational brain knew my children and I were all safe, my nervous system didn't. I still had to find a way to soothe and avoid triggering him. If I didn't, I was certain there would be consequences for people I loved.

He wasn't the only one who could trigger me. I was that woman behind the door, for example, when I heard the words of a then-presidential candidate. "I can do whatever I want," Trump said on that bus, to a man who cheered him on. "Grab them by the pussy..." I listened as he tossed around those words like they had no more significance than the breath mints he popped into his mouth in case he couldn't help himself and started kissing a woman.

I can assure you they were much more than just words to the millions of women who have cried behind closed doors. To me, they were flashes of memory that reignited the rage.

I was "grabbed by the pussy" many, many times. It happened in the kitchen or in the laundry room, while I was reading a book, talking on the phone, or driving. It happened while I was vacuuming or taking a bath, while our children were looking the other way or while I was walking down the stairs.

The boundaries I tried so carefully to place around my body made little difference. No matter what I was doing or how willing a recipient I was, a hand would reach out like a flash before I could see it and protect myself.

"I need you to listen to me!" I screamed again and again. "I need you to stop doing that!" And then for a few days or weeks, he'd be contrite, appearing to respect my request. But before long, I'd be walking down the hallway, and he'd grab again, sending my body into recoil at a new assault. "*Please* don't do that anymore!" I'd say again, through clenched teeth. I kept hoping he'd listen. I kept hoping he'd get it—how offensive it was to me, how it made me feel violated. I hoped and hoped and hoped.

I researched things like low self-esteem, ADHD, borderline personality disorder, low impulse control, bipolar disorder, and attachment disorder, thinking that if I could understand it, I could help him fix whatever was causing the behaviour. I didn't want to be angry with him. I didn't even want to blame him, if there was a reasonable explanation for why it continued to happen. I just wanted it to stop. And I wanted to be treated like someone worth cherishing. Whenever I found information that seemed relevant, I urged him to read it, too.

I did similar research for myself, hoping I could find reasons for my reaction to his grabbing, or ways in which I could improve my communication and create alternatives to the patterns that repeated themselves again and again. I wondered if this was normal for a marriage, or maybe my body was always in a hypersensitive state because of my rape.

I played through every scenario and explanation again and again, but at the end of each I still arrived at the same truth. And I still ended up crying behind the door.

My truth is this: I hate being grabbed unexpectedly. I always have, and I believe I always will. I hate being caught off guard and having my space and boundaries violated. I hate it when my right to consent is taken away from me.

But it didn't stop. I don't know the reasons why, and I stopped trying to figure them out.

He grabbed until that final time when I dropped the stack of towels I was carrying and screamed so loudly the children ran to their rooms to hide.

He grabbed until I stopped trying to fix him, stopped trying to make excuses for him, stopped ignoring my own discomfort, and asked him to move out instead. The only boundary that seemed to work was the one that allowed me to lock the door behind him.

WHY DID it take so long to leave the marriage? Why did I spend twenty-two years crying behind the door? I've asked myself those questions a thousand times, and the answer is never simple.

I stayed because I believed our children were better off with two parents in the home, even if those parents weren't well suited for each other. I doubted and gaslit myself, thinking I must be exaggerating and that it really wasn't that bad. I stayed because there were many times when he was good to me and to our children, and we were happy, so maybe the hard times weren't something to concern myself about. I kept hanging on to the fantasy that, if he could just find the right therapy or build his self-confidence, the loving and kind version of him would show up more consistently. I also stayed because of my own lack of self-love—deep down, I didn't believe I had the right to expect anything better. On top of that, there were all those things on my metaphorical Velcro dress—the belief that divorce is a sin and that a woman is meant to sacrifice herself in service to others.

Instead of leaving, I learned to dissociate and shut down all the ways my body was telling me to go.

In the end, there was one reason that trumped all the others: I stayed out of a belief that it was the best way to minimize potential harm to our children. I thought my years of practice in being hypervigilant would keep the situation safe and manageable so nobody would get hurt. If we were divorced and the children spent time in his home without me, I would have less ability to manage the situation for them. Also... what if a divorce triggered another suicide attempt? I knew that I would feel responsible if my daughters had to live with that.

What I couldn't see at the time was that the safety I was trying to create was a mirage, and my children knew it.

I hoped I could hold it all together at least until our daughters had graduated from high school. But then I started to see patterns of my own behaviour show up in my daughter's relationship with her boyfriend and I realized, with a sinking feeling, that I was passing down exactly what I didn't want them to face in future relationships. I watched her tend to his emotional needs at the expense of her own and knew I couldn't help her see the folly of that choice if I didn't stop doing it myself.

Just before Julie graduated, and five years before Madeline did, I asked M to move out of the house, letting go of the delusion that the world was mine to hold together.

A COUPLE of years after the divorce I finally recognized my codependency in the marriage. Despite the questions I'd asked multiple therapists, despite the number of books I'd read to try to understand what was going on, I was blind to how attached I was to my role as caregiver and fixer. The only clue I got was from the therapist we saw together when I told M I wanted him to move out of the house. She referred to me as the "overfunctioning" partner, and when I started to give M advice about when and how to find a place to live, she stopped me and said, "You're going to let him figure that out himself."

During the marriage, I'd read several articles about codependency and had even bought the book *Codependent No More* by Melody Beattie, but the label just didn't seem to fit. M wasn't an alcoholic, and much of the literature is about codependency with addicts, so it was hard to find myself in it. I never finished the book. Then one day, after the divorce, I heard somebody talking about codependency in a new way, and the light suddenly went on. I took the book off my shelf, and this time it all made sense.

According to *Psychology Today*, codependency is "a dysfunctional relationship dynamic where one person assumes the role of 'the giver,' sacrificing their own needs and well-being for the sake of the other, 'the taker.'" A codependent becomes so attached to their role as rescuer and helper that they can't imagine themselves outside that role and they can't imagine the other person surviving without them. They find it hard to set boundaries and be assertive, because they believe that if they do, the precarious world they're holding on their shoulders might crumble and people will get hurt.

Sadly, a codependent person becomes so hyperfocused on fixing another person's behaviour and solving their problems for them that it becomes like an addiction that they can't break free from. While a codependent becomes resentful of the ways the other person is ruining their life, they are also often afraid of the other person's healing because then their identity as rescuer will cease to be relevant.

> Ever since people first existed, they have been doing all the things we label "codependent." They have worried themselves sick about other people. They have tried to help in ways that didn't help. They have said yes when they meant no. They have tried to make other people see things their way. They have bent over backward to avoid hurting people's feelings and, in so doing, have hurt themselves. They have been afraid to trust their feelings. They have believed lies and then felt betrayed. They have wanted to get even and punish others. They have felt so angry they wanted to kill. They have struggled for their rights while other people said they didn't have any. They have worn sackcloth because they didn't believe they deserved silk.

Dr. Stephen Karpman's Drama Triangle sheds further light on my understanding of codependency. There are three roles on the Drama Triangle: victim, rescuer, and persecutor. The victim's narrative is "poor me." It's difficult for them to make decisions, solve problems, achieve insight, or take pleasure in life because they feel helpless, victimized, oppressed, and ashamed. The rescuer's narrative is "let me help." They constantly intervene on behalf of the victim, trying to save them from harm while ignoring their own needs. They fail to see that by offering short-term fixes, they enable victims to stay dependent. The persecutor's narrative is "it's all your fault." They are controlling, blaming, critical, oppressive, angry, authoritarian, rigid, and superior. They blame the victim and criticize the behaviour of the rescuer.

Each of us has a position on the triangle that we most gravitate toward. In a codependent relationship, a longstanding pattern emerges, but all of us can cycle through the positions at any given time. After M's second suicide attempt, for example, I had moments when I felt victimized by it, moments when I was angry and blamed him for ruining my life, and moments when I tried to rescue him.

Witnessing our relationship patterns can help us break the cycle of the Drama Triangle and set ourselves free. The people we have been perpetually stuck on the triangle with might try to pull us back into the loop, but we can choose not to join them there. In *The Power of TED: The Empowerment Dynamic*, David Emerald suggests that we can choose to step onto a new triangle where the victim becomes the creator (becoming empowered to take generative action), the rescuer becomes the coach (using inquiry, curiosity, and deep listening to support others in discovering what is best for them), and the persecutor becomes the challenger (inspiring others to reach for the highest good of all involved).

Why does a person become codependent and why does the Drama Triangle become such a familiar, well-ingrained pattern? The literature points toward childhood trauma and dysfunctional family patterns, and I can see the throughlines that suggest that to be true for me. I believe, though, that there's something bigger and more systemic that the experts often overlook. Codependency is rooted in behaviour and relationship patterns that are sanctioned by a patriarchal culture and religion. It's on all of our Velcro clothing. Those socialized as men aren't given sufficient tools to develop healthy relationships with their emotions, and those socialized as women are taught to do emotional labour on behalf of the entire family. We witness these patterns in our childhood, and we assume the roles before we know what we're doing. Then culture and religion reinforce and reward those behaviours until they become well ingrained.

To simply see and name the codependency without naming the larger pattern and the system that teaches and reinforces it can be victim blaming, something I'm trying to avoid doing to myself. Is it fair to blame an actor for playing a role onstage that she's spent many years training for, under the tutelage of a team of directors, when she was offered no clear alternatives for how to play that role?

Yes, I was codependent, but I was also doing the best I knew how to do given my socialization and the tools I had available to me. I was fulfilling the expectations placed on me to be a good wife and Good Christian Woman. I was trying to find love and security and trying to build a home where those things would be available for my children.

RECENTLY, I SPENT a weekend with my sister-in-law, driving around the western part of Ontario and the eastern part of Manitoba. She wanted to revisit some of the places that held her childhood memories, and I was game to accompany and support her. On the final day, we were on our way to a summer camp she'd attended, close to Whiteshell Provincial Park, when the memories being relived were suddenly mine instead of hers. We drove through a place where I knew I'd once spent a weekend in my mid-twenties, when I was newly dating the man I'd marry, but I had only vague memories of it.

Suddenly, though, my body remembered. When I spotted a familiar cabin, my body grew tense, and my brain started to buzz. Emotions flooded me and I lost all focus, barely able to speak. My sister-in-law, a therapist who is well versed in trauma, understood what was going on and asked if I wanted to stop. At first I said, "No, keep going," but an hour later, on our way back down that same road, I started weeping as we approached the cabin again. "Pull over," I said, in a strangled voice. I jumped out of the car and started pacing up and down the road. As I wept, my body shook, and I whispered to myself again and again, "You are safe now. You are safe now." Finally, with deep breaths, I brought my body back to stillness.

I still have little conscious memory of what happened at that cabin when I was in my twenties. I know that it was the first time I went away for a weekend with M and his friends. I vaguely remember there was drinking, boating, and knee-boarding.

The only specific memory I have was on the way to the cabin, when a friend and I were driving behind the vehicle M and his friends were in. One of them threw a beer can out the window, and my heart sank when I realized that they were not only drinking while driving, but they were littering. I shut down my disappointment, though, and said nothing. I was an awkward twenty-something who hadn't shaken the good-girl instincts of a religious childhood but who longed to be seen as interesting, cool, and worth hanging out with.

I don't know specifically how he treated me that weekend, because that memory remains elusive, but I remember enough weekends after that, when we were with his friends, when I tried hard to fit in and didn't value myself enough to recognize that "fitting in" was the equivalent of "losing myself."

I remember that there was an edge to his jokes when alcohol was involved. I remember walking away from the campfire one night, during another weekend of camping, in tears because I felt invisible to him. He found me later and apologized, but it was far from the last time it happened.

As I stood there on that road, thirty years after I'd first been there, I suddenly knew with crystal clarity that whatever happened at that cabin that weekend, it was the place where I abandoned myself to the relationship. It was a pivotal moment when I chose to prioritize my hunger for belonging over trust in my own body. I so wanted to be found worthy by a man that I shut down the instinct that was telling me I was not safe. That was the moment I started orienting my life around his dysfunction and abandoned my own boundaries in service to his pain. Rather than a specific incident, the self-abandonment was what my body brought to my attention.

I didn't know I could ask for better. I didn't know I was worthy of more. I'd waited so long to be loved that I thought this was what love looked and felt like.

If I could split my life in two, starting at that moment, I wonder what would have come if I'd turned the car around and chosen differently.

NOT LONG AGO, a friend asked me if I'd forgiven M, and I had to pause to think about it because I realized I didn't entirely know what forgiveness was or what markers I should look for that would indicate I'd arrived there.

I didn't hate him, and I believed he was better off being released from our unhealthy marriage, just as I was, so that we could both find more healing and less codependency, but there was a time when true forgiveness felt blocked by the pain I was still carrying. In retrospect, my lack of forgiveness revealed a continued unhealthy attachment to the dysfunction at the centre of our marriage. In trying to step off the Drama Triangle, I'd simply moved positions—from rescuer to victim and persecutor—and then justified those positions because I was still defining myself by my attachment to the pain.

With trauma so tightly woven into the threads of the story, from much further back than the moment we each said "I do," forgiveness feels rather nebulous and hard to pin down. Early on, I associated forgiveness too closely with reconciliation and lowered boundaries, and that didn't feel safe enough for me, so I prioritized my own healing and self-love instead.

For many years, I abandoned myself and undervalued my own needs and emotions, the way I'd so often seen modelled by women in the lineage before me. A rush to forgiveness felt like more of the same, so I didn't put pressure on myself to get there before I'd done enough healing work. First, I needed to be honest about the pain, honest about the ways my boundaries had been violated, and honest about the ways I'd stifled my own needs. Once those things were brought into the light, I could begin to heal them and not be so trapped in the trauma my body still carried (or so attached to the Drama Triangle).

I now believe that forgiveness is about finally becoming less attached to the pain, less attached to the role of rescuer, persecutor, or victim, and less attached to blame. I believe it's the simple yet hard-won act of letting go and living a more liberated life. It's what allows us to move from the Drama Triangle to The Empowerment Dynamic.

Yes, I forgive him. I'm not hanging on to this pain, or the anger once attached to it, and I don't need to see him suffer to somehow make the world right again. I see my role in the dysfunctional bond we were both part of and I want to be as free as I can be from all of it.

TWICE I'VE sat in women's circles with friends whose teenage sons had been accused of sexually inappropriate behaviour with girls. I watched as both moms wrestled with how to support their sons as they navigated the justice system, and once

I sat in the hallway outside the courtroom with one of them while she waited to get called in to testify.

Neither of these moms claimed that their son was entirely innocent, and everyone in our circle had empathy for the girls who'd experienced harm, and we wanted them to be believed and well cared for. What was also clear, though, was that the justice system wasn't serving anyone well in these situations— not the girls who deserved to be treated better and not the boys who needed to learn how to treat girls better. The justice system was built for punitive purposes, for proving one person wrong and another person right, and not for transformation, restoration, or healing. (It's the cultural manifestation of the Drama Triangle.) Instead of offering meaningful guidance and accountability that might transform these teenage boys into young men who understood consent and knew how to be respectful of women, the justice system reduced them to criminals and heaped the kind of shame and fear on them that could make them even less equipped for future relationships.

Beyond the justice system, the responsibility rests in our culture, our education systems, our schools, our communities, and our families to bring up and teach boys to understand consent. Instead of outsourcing the problem to the justice system and simply punishing the ways in which toxic masculinity manifests itself in these young boys, we need to get to the source, deconstruct the patriarchy, unravel the ways in which it lives in all of us, and then create healthy alternatives.

I share the story of these two young men because it relates to how I feel about the harm done in my marriage. While accountability is important in abuse situations, for myself, I am more interested in healing and transformation than I am in the kind of justice that would reattach either of us to the Drama Triangle. Though naming the abusive behaviour felt important during my healing process, when I needed more clarity about the boundaries I deserved to have, I've always felt somewhat ambivalent about calling it an "abusive marriage," because that feels too binary and reductive and doesn't fully encompass the complexity of the dysfunctions and maladaptive behaviour patterns we both needed to heal and transform.

At this point in my healing journey, I choose to spend my energy working toward a future where both men and women are more effectively supported in their emotional, sexual, and spiritual development so that we all know more about consent, boundaries, trauma, and harm in relationships. I want my daughters to know that they have a right to boundaries, and I want them to live in a world where repair and restorative justice become the focus whenever harm is done. I also want their male peers to know how to find love in healthy ways.

Sadly, my former husband and I both brought our brokenness into the marriage. We each tried to get our needs met in maladaptive ways, and those unmet needs poked at the other person's unmet needs and hooked us into the triangle. It wasn't just that his pain got projected onto me—I projected mine onto him as well.

I trust that the best way to live in peace is to release us both from the burden of guilt for all the ways that we hurt each other and didn't value ourselves. I no longer blame him, and I wish him liberation and love in the future. I hope that he finds happiness.

Similar to my rape story, I want to find space in this narrative for all of the wounded to be healed. Just like my rapist, I know that my former husband carried trauma in his body that he didn't know how to hold. As the poet Andrea Gibson said recently on Facebook, "I never found a genuine way to heal until I was genuinely rooting for everybody's healing, including the people whose poor decisions I was healing from."

Ultimately, though, this story is not about my former husband. What feels most important to me is that I learn to forgive myself and tell the truth to myself. In those twenty-four years after I abandoned myself at that cabin, I betrayed myself many, many times, and that feels almost harder to bear than the ways that he hurt me. Since the marriage ended, I've been learning to forgive myself one step at a time, and I've been learning to give myself the protection and care I didn't receive from those I most expected it from. I'm letting go of the healing fantasy and doing my best to practice loving myself in the ways I always longed to be loved.

Ironically, a person whose nervous system has been on alert because the world proved itself to be unsafe will often accept, and even gravitate toward, unsafe environments—even ones where they are being mistreated—because that's what feels familiar. Veterans returning from war zones often feel less at ease in the comfort of their homes than they did in places where their lives were genuinely at risk. In a similar way, I accepted the lack of safety in my marriage because it felt familiar to my activated nervous system, and I attached myself to the role of rescuer because it gave my life a misguided sense of purpose.

MY FIRST VISIT to the woman crying behind the door, when I discovered her at the Weisman Art Museum shortly after my marriage unravelled, marked a new beginning for me. I was drawn to her because I *was* her, but I didn't yet know how to reach through the door to reclaim her. Gradually, I learned how to call her back from exile, to let her know that she didn't need to abandon herself, close the door, keep people's secrets, sacrifice her own needs, and cry alone. Gradually, I learned that she was the one I most needed to care for, and that it wasn't my job to hold the world together for everybody else. Gradually, I learned to retrain my nervous system and find comfort in safer places.

When I first wrote this story, it ended on a triumphant note. "The door is now wide open," it said, "and her story has been told. I will not abandon her again. I will not keep anyone's secrets at the expense of the woman behind the door, and I won't let anyone hurt her like that again." I wanted it to be over. I wanted there to be a clean ending. But then something happened that sent me behind the door again, and I realized that there will likely always be a small part of me that feels she needs to hide behind that door. During the editorial process of this book, I once again found myself worrying about who I was responsible for protecting in keeping this story a secret. On an airplane, shortly after a meeting about the book, I spent much of the flight trying to keep my seatmates and the flight attendants from seeing that I was fighting tears.

When you carry a story like this for so many years—telling no one because of the risks to people you love and because of the shame it invokes in you—it's not easy to release it. In the end, though, I believe that freedom for the woman behind the door is also freedom for others like her, and even for the people who hurt her. I share this story in service to our collective liberation and healing. For anyone reading this who feels like that woman behind the door right now, know that I am standing on the other side, ready to offer you tissues and tea. And for anyone crying behind a door because you relate more to my former husband's side of this story, I can say now that I would also offer you tissues and tea. (A few years ago, in fact, I was able to do just that for a young man who admitted to having done similar harm, and both of us received healing from that encounter.)

Setting ourselves free is not a one-time thing, as I once hoped it might be. It's an ongoing process involving a lot of self-compassion and courage that I will keep working at for the rest of my life.

I forgive the woman behind the door, and I love her and am determined to no longer betray or abandon her. I will set her free as often as I need to. And I will set free the people who hurt her, too.

REFLECTION QUESTIONS

WHETHER OR NOT you've ever been married or in a long-term relationship, there are likely ways in which you have had to let go of expectations from your early life and live with the shattering of your dreams. Perhaps you have also been in complicated relationships where there were patterns of abuse and/or codependency. Perhaps you have spent time crying behind closed doors.

1 In what ways did this story resonate for you? What emotions did it bring up for you?

2 This chapter is mostly about my own choices in the marriage. How might you be making similar choices in an unhealthy relationship?

3 In which relationships might you need to develop healthier boundaries?

4 What old messages do you carry that might be keeping you in unhealthy situations?

5 Who are you afraid of letting down if you need to make a hard decision about your life?

6 What cultural shifts might be needed so that fewer people feel trapped in unhealthy relationships?

7   In the Karpman Drama Triangle, there are three positions—victim, rescuer, and persecutor. How does this apply to your relationships, and which position feels most familiar to you?

8   What can you do to step away from the Drama Triangle and into The Empowerment Dynamic (creator, coach, challenger)?

9   What is your hope for future relationships (or the way you want current ones to evolve)?

5

This Fat Body

HAVEN'T LOOKED in a mirror in four days. I'm staying at my friend Mary's house in Costa Rica, where I've come to work on this portion of the book, and there are no mirrors in her guest bedroom or bathroom. There's a decorative mirror in the living room, but I haven't bothered to look in it. At first, I considered using my phone's camera as a mirror, but now I've gotten used to the idea of not seeing myself. While I peer into my interior landscape as honestly as I can, there's a certain freedom in not concerning myself with what others see when they look at me. I have spent too much of my life caring about what people see. Now I want to know what it's like to live without this concern, and what it's like to love my body wholeheartedly and unconditionally, apart from the gaze of others.

"YOUR BODY is a temple," I was taught in my growing-up years. That's a potentially beautiful sentiment, but in my religious context, it was primarily interpreted to mean that, as a place where God resides, you shouldn't do anything shameful with your body because then God wouldn't be able to dwell inside you. Be modest with how much of it you expose. Don't defile it with alcohol or drugs. Keep it pure until marriage. Don't expose yourself to pornography or anything that might make your body feel desires you shouldn't feel. Don't touch yourself in a sensual way. Don't wear make-up or get body piercings. Don't dance. Don't enjoy too much pleasure or give in to desire, especially when that desire involves anything erotic. Don't be slothful, lazy, or fat.

Ironically, when you work so hard to keep your body from shamefulness, the shame grows like a weed and roots itself even more deeply in your body. (And I would dare to say that shame is not the decor of a temple in which God resides.) Like a strangler fig that wraps itself around a healthy tree until the tree can barely see the sun, shame shapes your identity and becomes the lens through which you see yourself when you look in the mirror.

There were subtle things that taught me that my body was shameful. I picked it up from the way my mom looked at herself in the mirror with dislike and disappointment and how she scrambled to make herself presentable when company came. It was present in the comments my dad made when my skirt was too short or my neckline plunged too deeply and the disapproving looks or judgmental comments when people on the street or on TV were too scantily clad. And then there was the fact that sex was strongly forbidden until that day when, with a ring on your finger and with no practice and heaps of prior shame, it was supposed to be easy and magical. All of these things and more were attached to my Velcro dress from an early age—a dress that kept my body well hidden.

In church I learned to hide my body in shame, and in school I quickly learned that my brain gave me value in ways that my body didn't. Consistently among the top students of my class, I received the affirmations I craved when I excelled at academics. Although I enjoyed sports and joined nearly every team that I could in our small town, I never excelled at any of them, and so I poured most of my effort into the kind of grades that would make the grownups proud. When I graduated from grade nine, before heading off to high school in the larger town half an hour away, I was given the award for highest academic achievement. Less and less, after that, did my body merit any meaningful attention. I hid its deficiencies and shamefulness while my brain led the way. In university, I studied theatre but found that my body, which had never been allowed to express itself through movement, was awkward and clumsy onstage. I soon learned that I was better at writing plays than performing in them, so I stuck with what my brain could do without my body's full presence.

That became a familiar pattern that informed the shape of my adult life. Years later, my friend Tu Bears, an Elder from the Choctaw Nation, told me that her grandfather had said that white people seem to live like their heads are cut off from their bodies, and I recognized that, at least in my case, he was right. My brain mattered. My body didn't.

SEX. IT CAN BE a minefield for even the most liberated person, and I was about as far from liberated as one can be without falling off the far end of the bell curve. I didn't date at all in high school or Bible college. I was shy and awkward, especially where boys were concerned, and I was completely baffled by the kind of flirting that came so naturally for many of my peers. Partly because of the way I hid my body behind my brain, boys were often either intimidated by me or confused by me, and so I didn't get asked out and certainly didn't see it as a possibility that I could be the one to initiate a relationship. The whole world of male-female relationships was a mystery, and I was far too repressed to consider a female-female one.

The closest I came to any hint of intimacy in those days was with the second cousin who found an excuse to kiss me while playing a game in junior high, and the high school friend who asked me to be his date at the last minute for the graduation dinner (though I was forbidden from attending the dance).

That's how innocent I was when, at twenty-two, my body was violated by a stranger who climbed through my apartment window. Before that, I had known no physical touch other than my mother's, or an occasional hug from a friend or family member. I don't remember even discovering that I could pleasure myself before that—it was just too shameful to consider.

I was shocked and dismayed at the way my body responded to the touch of my rapist on my clitoris. How could arousal be possible in the middle of such fear? And yet it happened. That's the first time I discovered that I lived in a sexual body, with shame and trauma so intertwined with sexuality that it took me years to even begin to untangle them.

In the pink bathtub of the apartment I shared with my sister for the two years following my rape, I, belatedly and with much secrecy and shame, began to experiment with how it felt to touch my body. It felt good and bad all at the same time. At a university party around that time, I let a classmate kiss me and slip his tongue into my mouth. I wasn't attracted to him, but I wanted to know what it felt like to be kissed by someone who didn't smell like rubbing alcohol and glue. Then, in that apartment with the pink bathtub, while my sister was at our parents' house for the weekend, I invited another classmate home after a party and let him take off my shirt and bra and touch my breasts. That's as far as I was willing to go, though, and the next morning I felt dirty and ashamed. I made sure the apartment showed no signs of anyone else having been there so that my sister wouldn't ask any questions.

A year later, a work friend said he wanted to introduce me to his cousin. It should have been a red flag that, when my friend called him from work to talk to him about meeting me, he responded with, "I'm here waiting, with nothing on but a condom." But I agreed to meet him with a group of friends at a bar a few nights later. He asked me out the next week and we started dating. I ignored one red flag after another, because he was funny and smart and I wanted someone to love me. He appreciated my body and I thought that's what I needed to heal.

Hindsight is twenty-twenty, and now I see the baggage I was carrying into that relationship. I didn't know how to receive touch; M didn't know how to give it in a way that respected boundaries; and I thought that when my body recoiled, it was because I wanted to wait until marriage to go all the way. I had no idea how to read the signs my body was sending me. And I was surprised to find out that, even after marriage, my body still regularly recoiled.

I have written, in an earlier chapter, about how fraught our sex life was and how much it revolved around his insatiable neediness, but I must also say that some of what made it fraught was my body's lack of willingness to receive his touch. For a man already tortured with abandonment issues and low self-esteem, this added fuel to the fire. I tried hard to be willing, and there were times when it was better than others, but I can only remember two times in our twenty-two years of marriage when we had what I'd consider to be really good sex—once after skinny-dipping at the beach where we had a camper parked for the summer, and once in a hotel room in Quebec City when I invited him along on a business trip. Both times, I was sufficiently intoxicated to loosen up.

About six years before the marriage ended, I started to fantasize about being with a woman. I wasn't sure whether it was out of genuine, awakened desire, or if it was because it felt less like I was cheating on him in my mind, or if it was easier to imagine sex feeling safe with a woman. Whatever the reason, I let myself entertain the fantasy. It gave me some escapism during the troubling final years of the marriage.

It took me several years after the divorce to even begin to consider being with another person, because that kind of intimacy felt far too fraught, and I still had no idea how to flirt. I was also cautious not to bring anyone into my daughters' lives too early, so I waited until it felt like the right time before I opened the door to the possibility. About four years after the divorce, when my therapist asked if it might feel safer being with a woman, I admitted that I'd been considering it. "You travel a lot, right?" she asked. "Why not hook up with someone in a city far from home where you might experiment without anyone else knowing?" What she suggested felt too far outside my comfort zone, but I told her I'd at least consider which baby steps I was willing to take.

That night, I told my daughters that the future might include me dating a woman, and they responded with delight. (They are all queer themselves.) I downloaded a lesbian dating app and created a profile, but I panicked the moment someone started chatting with me and quickly deleted it.

Several months later, my friendship with a woman who lives in another city became increasingly intimate. She'd divorced her husband shortly after I'd divorced mine, and we'd supported each other through many of the related challenges. We spent a few days together at a cabin and, reaching for her hand on the couch one day, I asked her if she might consider the possibility that we could take our relationship to another level of intimacy. She said she wasn't entirely closed to the idea, but wasn't ready for it yet.

For the next nine months, we chatted weekly on Zoom, and then one day, a little shyly, she told me that she was open to the idea now and asked if I'd go on a date with her. We agreed to meet in a city halfway between us to see whether something might evolve. Though we were somewhat awkward, we had our first (and second) sexual encounter that weekend, and it was lovely and tender. Perhaps most importantly for me, my body felt safe and trusting under her touch, and it didn't recoil. Plus, I felt little shame.

After meeting one more time, we both agreed that there wasn't quite enough between us to sustain a relationship. Since then, we have returned to our friendship and more sporadic Zoom calls. We have both expressed gratitude for the experience we shared. More than anything, I am grateful for the way that she helped me discover that touch can be safe and that my body doesn't recoil if I'm with someone whose touch I trust.

It was only very recently that I put together the pieces and remembered that my very first sexual experience was with a girl. As awkward preteens, a friend and I experimented with each other's bodies, skin against skin under the covers, telling ourselves we were simply trying to figure out what we'd eventually do with our husbands. Our tender exploration ended abruptly, though, when her mom discovered us naked in bed together, and we were both filled with so much shame that neither of us ever brought it up again.

When I think back to that time, long before I was raped and ended up in a sexually unhealthy marriage, and moments before we internalized the shame of our parents, I remember how pleasurable it was to have my body touched by a girl.

"WHAT IS your body telling you?" When my therapist asked me that, shortly after my divorce and long before the relationship with my friend evolved, I looked at her as though she were speaking a foreign language. "What do you mean?" I asked, baffled by the question. "Is your body sending you any messages about what it wants and needs?" she continued. I shook my head, trying not to be annoyed by her odd line of inquiry. I had no frame of reference for communicating with my body—nothing about her questions made sense to me. "Maybe you should start asking it," she coaxed.

I took a deep breath. "I don't know how to do that. I don't know how to hear its answer." And then, because my intellect is my first line of defence when something puzzles me: "Is there a book I can read that can teach me?"

"No," she said, gently. "You're not going to read books to navigate your way through this one. You're just going to have to practice spending time with your body. Ask it what it wants and needs, and then pause until you have an answer. Once it knows you're listening, it's going to start talking to you." I tried not to let her see just how annoyed I was with her answer.

At the end of the session, she pointed out that something had changed during our meeting. "When we first started talking, you were coughing quite a lot and now you're not. Perhaps your body is already beginning to respond to your willingness to finally listen to it."

As much as I was resistant to what she was offering me—I drove home wondering if I'd wasted money on such woo-woo advice—I suspected there was truth in it. I wasn't good at listening to my body. Years of dissociation had taught me to numb and distrust its sensations and make decisions based mostly in my head.

Over the coming weeks, I warmed to the idea and started looking for ways to begin having a healthier relationship with my body. I booked reiki sessions and massages, joined movement classes, and started walking more regularly. Sometimes I'd sit with my journal and write, "Body, what do you need today?" at the top of the page and then wait to see if an answer would show up. Most importantly, I started learning about the impact trauma had had on my body and got better at recognizing the signals when it didn't feel safe.

There were two physical things that kept showing up for most of the years of my marriage—restless legs syndrome and frequent yeast infections. The restless legs syndrome started in my first pregnancy. The muscles in my legs would suddenly feel twitchy, with an overwhelming compulsion to run. At first it only happened when I was pregnant, but then it became a regular—sometimes even nightly—occurrence. There was no scientific explanation for it, only theories.

I don't remember when the yeast infections started, but I know that they became more and more frequent further into the marriage. A yeast infection usually made sex painful, which meant I said no even more frequently than usual, so it was a source of great frustration for my husband and he often wondered whether I was lying when I said I had one.

Quite abruptly, when the marriage ended and I was finally sleeping alone in a bedroom that now felt safe, both of those things stopped, almost completely. Both, I've since discovered, can be traced to trauma, rooted in the body's sympathetic nervous system. My body was trying to protect me from the sex I didn't want to have and to escape a bed that didn't feel safe.

To say that I've resolved the old patterning that the therapist pointed out would be an overstatement—it's still very much a work in progress. A few years ago, I broke my shoulder in a freak accident that felt related to embodied trauma. That afternoon, I'd had a difficult conversation with some people who mean a lot to me and who I was in conflict with at the time. I came off that Zoom call feeling shaky but had to turn my attention to my daughters, since I'd promised to take them to a restaurant for supper. When we were getting ready to leave, M showed up at the door and pulled me aside to talk to me privately. Before I could let him know I wasn't in the mood for a conversation with him, he said, without warning, "Those stories that are coming out about the way Harvey Weinstein treated women—is that the way I treated you?" I was dumbfounded and speechless. "Yes," I finally said, unwilling to lie to make him feel better. "I'm sorry," he said, casually. "I was an idiot." And then he rushed quickly past the apology and started expounding on how much more horrible Weinstein had been to far more women. I was silent, giving nothing in return for what felt like a meaningless and poorly timed apology. He left shortly thereafter. My brain buzzed and my body went numb with what had just been off-loaded onto me in such a casual way, when I was already feeling wobbly from the Zoom call. Somehow I got through supper with my daughters and then headed straight to the bathtub where I thought I could find enough privacy to release some tears. Uncharacteristically, I locked the bathroom door, but then Julie pounded on the door because she wanted access to her cosmetics before going out for the evening. Resentfully, I stood up in the bathtub, reached too far for the doorknob (rather than climbing out of the tub), slipped, and crashed to the floor.

It took months to discover that I had an avulsion fracture, and months more to heal it. I reflected often about how I'd broken a shoulder just when it felt like too much emotional weight was being dumped on my shoulders. A few days after I was injured, I went to a friend's birthday party, where we were supposed to dress in superhero costumes. I pinned a sign onto my arm sling that said, "Tired Supermom who injured her shoulder after carrying the weight of the world on it."

Despite the pain and frustration of that broken shoulder, an experience like that taught me that my body has had to hold a lot and I need to keep finding healthier ways to process and release what it doesn't need to carry anymore. Plus, I need to get better and better at erecting healthy boundaries that honour my body so that I can be free.

I keep trying to live into the belief that when my body is loved, well cared for, and more protected, every part of me benefits. I'm getting much better at that. Today, for example, the words are flowing onto this page with greater ease because last night, Mary took me to the natural hot springs here (her farm in Costa Rica is close to a volcano) and then we ate a delicious meal at a new Korean restaurant. This morning, before I started writing, I turned on the music and danced. I will do the same later in the day when my body starts to feel weary from so much sitting. Or perhaps I'll take a nap. A happier body, I'm learning, makes for a happier mind and spirit.

I WAS THIRTEEN and we were bowling with our small church group. A woman whose children I often babysat and whose husband was our youth leader stood up to bowl, and my mom leaned over to whisper in my ear conspiratorially, "When I go stand beside her, check who looks fatter from the back, her or me." I froze. Before Mom sat back down, I disappeared into the bathroom and then found another place to sit until it was my turn to bowl. I don't remember ever answering her question.

Like most young girls, I learned early that fatness is shameful. My mom never learned to love her own body and expressed on her deathbed that she was worried about what people would think of her when her body was lying in the coffin. She worried all her life about getting fat (though, ironically, her deathbed concern was that she'd become too skinny) and that was passed down to me. When I look back at pictures of myself as a teenager, I realize that I probably had some body dysmorphia back then, because I was convinced I was fat, even though the pictures show me as average sized.

I am fat now—fatter than I've ever been in my life. I have battled fatness throughout much of my adult life, believing, like my mom did before me, that I'd only be worthy of the love I craved if I were thin.

There are mixed messages in my subconscious, though. At two of the thinnest points in my adult life, tragedy happened to my body, leaving behind some residual messages that tell my body it is safer to be fat. When I was twenty-two, I was training to be part of a relay team for a triathlon, cycling thirty or forty kilometres a day on my sleek silver Miele bicycle. I was in the best physical shape of my life, had a beautiful golden tan from so many hours in the sun, and felt vibrant and alive. Two days before the triathlon, at the peak of my fitness, I was raped. I backed out of the triathlon and was replaced on the team by another cyclist. I started gaining weight not long after that.

Several years later, after Julie was born, I lost a lot of the weight I'd gained over the years through an unusual but effective church-based diet program called Weigh Down (that, among other things, convinced women it was God's will that they be thin). I felt really good about the way my body finally looked and was determined to stay that weight. Then I got pregnant with our third child, and he was born dead. I started gradually gaining weight after the pregnancy ended.

When I got divorced, I convinced myself (influenced by online health coaches) that once I was happier, my body would naturally slim down. The opposite happened. The happier I became and the more I healed the wounds left behind by the marriage, the more weight I put on.

Finally, I grew tired of being at war with my body and decided to stop trying to punish it into a more acceptable shape. In search of a better way, I followed the breadcrumbs on the internet and discovered several nutritionists and health experts who revealed that most of what we've been taught about the connection between thinness and health is wrong and that health is possible at any size. I also learned about the systemic oppression of fat bodies and discovered how much of the shame I carried was deliberately heaped on me by patriarchy, white supremacy, and capitalism. To create body hierarchies and give certain people more power, systems of dominance and control look for the bodies that can be marginalized. Fat bodies provide an easy target. Once those bodies are disempowered and full of shame, capitalism swoops in to make heaps of money off diet programs, exercise programs, supplements, and clothes that constrict the body and hide the shame.

Fat bodies live at the margins of culture. If clothing stores have plus-sized clothing at all, they're usually tucked into the nether regions of the store. Manufacturers of backpacks or fanny packs don't expect fat people to use their products, so they don't bother making the straps long enough. Few restaurants or hospital waiting rooms consider fat bodies when they select their chairs. Even those people and organizations who advocate on behalf of marginalized people tend to ignore fat bodies in their efforts to build equity. Why? Because, unlike other marginalized people, it is still assumed that fat people are to blame for their own misfortune and don't have a right to complain about the way the world mistreats them.

"Living in a female body," says Sonya Renee Taylor in *The Body Is Not an Apology*, "a Black body, an aging body, a fat body, a body with mental illness is to awaken daily to a planet that expects a certain set of apologies to already live on our tongues.

There is a level of 'not enough' or 'too much' sewn into these strands of difference."

Recently, I realized just how much internalized oppression I carry in this fat body. I noticed how difficult it is to advocate for my own rights to better treatment, better clothing options, fewer harmful assumptions made by medical professionals, et cetera, and how much shame fills me when I try. "It's your own fault so you don't deserve better," a voice in my head keeps telling me, every time I consider asking for what I need. "You put the food in your mouth that made your body fat, so you get to live with the consequences of those choices. Shame on you."

Perhaps, if I excavate deeply enough, to the origins of this belief system, it can be traced back to a religion that taught me that the punishment for my sins would be an eternity in hell. If my fat body is punishment for the sin of eating too much, it stands to reason that I have no right to expect anyone to treat this fat body well (another layer on my Velcro dress).

Religion, and my parents' fear that I might stray away from that religion, ingrained in me a belief that I have to earn love, that I have to prove my worthiness, and that, as long as I deviate from the acceptable path, I have no right to ask for my needs to be met or for anyone to protect me. I have no right to comfort, safety, or pleasure.

Gradually, I have chipped away at those beliefs, determined to offer my body love and tenderness no matter its shape or ability—to be unconditional in my self-affection. I am determined to rebel against any system that tells me I must look or move a certain way to be worthy of love. I am determined to turn away from and/or challenge any body shaming that I see in the media or on my friends' social media streams. It's not easy, and it's so counter-cultural it seems deviant.

One of the ways I've learned to love my body is to call it fat without holding "fatness" as a derogatory term. "Saying I'm fat is (and should be) the same as saying my shoes are black, the clouds are fluffy, and Bob Saget is tall," says Sonya Renee Taylor. "It's not good, it's not bad, it just is. The only negativity that this word carries is that which has been socially constructed around it ... We don't need to stop using the word fat, we need to stop the hatred that our world connects with the word fat."

Much has changed in the way I treat my body, but there's something more that I'm still unravelling, even as I write this— something that takes me even further on this healing journey, beyond objectification and toward integration. I'm not sure that it's enough to say, "I love my body." What I'm coming to believe instead is that I need to learn to love *with* my fat body and *in* my fat body. To say I love "it" is to treat my body as something "other," separate from my spirit and soul, inanimate and disengaged, like a piece of furniture or a tool. It's the same "body as resource" objectification that I talked about in the chapter about my rape.

This fat body is so much more—she is me. I do not exist without a body. I do not love without a body. I do not move in the world without a body. I am my body, and my body is me. Everything starts with that. Loving my body is loving me. To objectify my body is to sever me from myself.

This body that is me is beautiful, sensuous, and healthy. My body moves in the world with grace and passion and loves a good massage and a long soak in a hot tub. She (because there must be a pronoun that's better than "it") welcomes tender and generous touch and looks forward to her next sexual experience. She loves to float in the ocean or in a float tank. This fat body thrives on mountain hikes, bike rides, and canoe trips, and she wraps her arms around her children when they cry. This fat body aches sometimes and can't move in the way she once could, but she chooses not to fear the aging process ahead of her. This fat body holds trauma and can be easily triggered into maladaptive behaviour, but she is doing the best she can to heal. I am a good body, and I will be a good body even when I can't dance or bike anymore. This fat body is full of love and I am worthy of being loved.

Last year, I had the words of a Mary Oliver poem tattooed on my forearm where I can easily see them: "... let the soft animal of your body love what it loves." Though the "it" in that sentence no longer feels quite right, those words serve as a guide for me as I honour my own desire and practice loving with my whole body, heart, and soul. A soft animal feels much more alive and vibrant than a piece of furniture.

RECENTLY, AFTER a few years of doing healing work to nurture this emerging, radical love that lives in my body, I stumbled upon a queer-friendly, clothing-optional beach in a resort town where I was staying in Spain while finishing this book. When I first walked by, on the path along the cliff above the beach, I could feel the excitement in my body mount. "Do I dare to visit? Can I believe that my body is welcome there?"

The idea wouldn't leave me alone, and two days later, I threw a dress over my naked body, grabbed a towel, and headed to the beach. Though it took a while for me to settle (at first, I found myself in what seemed to be a gay-men-only section of the beach), I finally put down my towel, took off my dress, straightened my shoulders, and walked naked into the water.

And then I swam, floated, and played in the waves, completely naked and completely happy.

What I loved most about it was that I felt unremarkable on that beach. I wasn't too fat, too old, too saggy, or too pale. I was just another ordinary body among a lot of other ordinary bodies. Every one of us was beautifully imperfect. Some were disproportionately heavy on the top, some were heavier on the bottom, some were skinny, some were short, some were tall, some had saggy breasts, and some had smaller-than-average penises. I didn't see one "perfect" body on that whole beach—not a single one of us looked like we'd walked out of the pages of a magazine.

"They have sold us a lie," I thought, as I enjoyed so many versions of imperfect bodies. "They have convinced us to hold up an impossible ideal, to spend money trying to reach that ideal, and to punish ourselves for not reaching it. Not *one* of us looks like that when we take off all our clothes and stand naked on this beach."

Later, I lay on my towel under the sun, still naked and still in awe of the beautiful bodies around me. Tears welled up in my eyes. "I feel safe here," I thought. "Nobody is judging me. Nobody is sexualizing me. Nobody wants to harm my body. Nobody is even looking at me." Never in my wildest dreams did I expect to find safety for my hypervigilant body on a clothing-optional beach. Life is full of surprises.

TWICE DURING the year that my friend Randy was dying of ALS, I spent a few days in his home. On the first visit, he still had enough mobility that he could feed himself (with special utensils that were easier to grab) and pull himself to his feet to transfer from his wheelchair to the toilet (or to give me a hug).

During that first visit, he wanted to take me out for supper, so he made a reservation at one of his favourite places, an old church that's been converted into a pub. Randy and I have been in restaurants together many times over the years and, almost always, because he was older and male, the servers assumed he would be paying the bill and spoke more directly to him than to me. This time, though, because I was pushing him in his wheelchair and his voice was slurred, assumptions changed and the servers spoke more directly to me. Not surprisingly, they had been socialized to assume a disabled body has less value and agency (and was less able to communicate or make decisions) than one with no obvious disabilities.

On my second visit, Randy had lost almost all his mobility and much of his capacity for speech. He could move one hand only about five inches away from his body and could still turn his neck, but little else. He could no longer eat solid food and was being fed through a feeding tube. We could have only short conversations and I had to lean in with focused attention to understand him.

While with Randy on that second visit, knowing it would be my last time with him, I had a moment when the immensity of love for my friend nearly knocked me flat. I suddenly realized how little the quality or capacity of his body mattered to our friendship. It didn't matter if his body was young, old, thin, fat, disabled, ugly, out of shape, deformed, or incapable of movement. I loved him and will always love him. It was his beautiful spirit that shaped our friendship, and even when his body had little ability left, I still flew across the country to be with him.

I want to feel the same way about my own body. I want to believe in my body's absolute worthiness, regardless of ability, beauty, or thinness. I want to shed all the shame that's been layered onto this body, and I want to set myself free so that I can feel bountiful pleasure. When my body deteriorates into old age or illness, I want to treat myself as tenderly as I treated Randy in the months leading up to his death.

REFLECTION QUESTIONS

WHETHER OR NOT you are fat, I expect that elements of this story feel familiar to you. As I've discovered in leading retreats and online courses, some version of body shame seems to be present for every person I interact with. Reflect on your relationship with your own body and what messages you've received about the value of that body. Notice the way the systems you're part of (familial systems, cultural systems, religious systems) reinforce those messages and make it hard to find your way to self-love.

1   What do you love about your body? What shame do you carry about your body?

2   How do you feel about the sexual nature of your body? What messages did you learn in childhood that might still be shadowing your current belief about yourself?

3   I have intentionally chosen to adopt "fat" as a way to define my body because I believe, like so many fat-positive activists who influenced me, that "fat" should simply be a defining word with no negative charge, just like hair colour or eye colour. Which words have you used about yourself (or others have used about you) that might have a negative charge? Can these words be reclaimed, or are there other words that feel more neutral, or even empowering?

4   I had a late coming out as a queer person. In what ways do you still need to "come out" (not necessarily about sexual identity)? Are there aspects of who you are and what your body longs for that still hold too much shame to be spoken about publicly?

5   What is your body telling you?

6 Is there a way that you've lived with an expectation that, in the words of Sonya Renee Taylor, a "certain set of apologies" should already be "living on your tongue"?

7 What liberation do you need from systems that try to oppress and control your body?

8 What collective liberation is needed so that we can all live in freer bodies?

6

Intersections

A FEW YEARS AGO, I facilitated a retreat for the staff and board members of a non-profit in Winnipeg. At the retreat, we played Barnga, an inter-cultural learning game that gives people a little taste of the experience of what it feels like to be a "stranger in a strange land."

To play Barnga, people sit at tables in groups of four. Each group is given a simple set of rules and a deck of cards. After reading the rules, they play a couple of practice rounds. Once they're comfortable with the rules, they are instructed to play the rest of the game in silence, and the rule sheets are taken away. After fifteen or twenty minutes of playing in silence, the person who won at each table is invited to move to another table. The person who lost moves to a table in the opposite direction.

The game begins again, but what people don't realize until they've played a round or two with new players is that each table has a different set of rules. At some tables, ace is high and at others, it's low. At one table, diamonds are trump, at another, clubs are trump.

Newcomers to each table expect the rules to be the same, but after making a few mistakes and losing what they thought they'd won, they realize that the rules have changed. Because they were instructed to be silent, they have no shared language to ask questions that might help them understand what they're doing wrong. Around the room, confusion and frustration generally grow as people try to adapt to the new rules, and those at the table try to use hand gestures and other creative means to communicate what the newcomers are doing wrong.

After another fifteen or twenty minutes, the winners and losers move to new tables and another round begins. This time, the newcomers expect different rules and are more prepared to adapt. In this round, people usually try to communicate the rules to newcomers before the game starts.

This day, after playing for about forty-five minutes, we gathered in a sharing circle to debrief about the experience. Some shared that, even though they had stayed at their table and the rules didn't change, when someone else insisted on playing by different rules, they doubted themselves. Some even found themselves giving up their own rules entirely, even though they hadn't changed tables.

In the group of twenty people, there was one able-bodied cisgender white man and nineteen women and non-binary people of different races and abilities. "I just realized what I've done," the solitary man said, appalled at his sudden realization. "I was so confident that I knew the rules of the game and that others didn't that I took my own rules with me wherever I went and enforced them regardless of how other people were playing."

Everyone else at the tables he moved to adapted to his set of rules. Perhaps they doubted their own memory of the rules, perhaps they felt it more important to be peacekeepers, or perhaps their role in the organizational structure meant that they were used to adapting to this man's ideas. Whatever the case, they each acquiesced.

Unconsciously and without ill intent on his part, this man exerted his privilege and power in the room, probably thinking he was helping people by explaining the "right" rules to them. Possibly without recognizing it was happening, the others at those tables had their power taken away and their own culture and rules marginalized.

A WEEK after that retreat, I was reminded of how I, too, can be guilty of assuming other people are playing by the same rules I am. During that time, I was involved in hosting race relations conversations in Winnipeg. These evolved in response to an article in *Maclean's* magazine that named Winnipeg the most racist city in Canada. The article emerged soon after the murder of Tina Fontaine, a fifteen-year-old child from the Sagkeeng First Nation who was murdered and wrapped in plastic and tossed into the Red River after being sexually exploited in the city's core. The article, by Nancy Macdonald, recounted the stories of many Indigenous people who'd suffered from racism in the city. Macdonald's article was published around the same time as an inquest issued its findings regarding the death of Brian Sinclair, a forty-five-year-old Indigenous man who, after being ignored for thirty-four hours in an ER waiting room, died from an entirely treatable infection.

After the article caused a stir in Winnipeg and beyond, a group of us got together because we wanted to do something about it. I worked in partnership with Rosanna Deerchild, a Cree radio host who had unwillingly been made the poster child for this issue when her photo was used on the front cover of *Maclean's*, to host a series of events that we called Race for Peace.

In a blog post about the first event we hosted, I wrote that "we all felt like we'd been punched in the gut" when our city was labelled most racist.

That's when I discovered that I was "carrying my own rules." Several people pointed out that I was assuming that my response to the article was an accurate depiction of how *everyone* felt. By doing so, I was erasing the experiences of the very people whose stories had been featured in the article.

Not everyone felt like they'd been punched in the gut by the article. Many felt a sense of relief that the stories of racism were finally coming out in the mainstream press. In the critique of my blog post, one person said that my comment about feeling punched in the gut made *her* feel punched in the gut. Another reflected that mine was a "settler's narrative." These readers pointed out that my perspective, as someone whose lineage was among the colonizing settlers of this country, was doing further harm rather than contributing to the healing of our city.

I was mortified. In my efforts to enter this conversation with humility, I had inadvertently done the opposite of what I'd intended. Like the man in the Barnga game, I'd assumed that everyone was playing by the same set of rules. After losing a night of sleep over it, I updated the blog post, apologized, and thanked those who'd challenged me.

NOT LONG after that, I attended a weekly sharing circle at the Indigenous Family Centre. Though I'd been there before and knew I was welcome, I was nervous. I was afraid I didn't belong, afraid I looked too much like the oppressor with my white skin, and afraid I'd once again be confronted by my own biases and shown more evidence of how I carry the colonizer's rules with me. Determined to face those fears, though, and trying to be willing to receive the hard information I needed to face to make a meaningful contribution to reconciliation, I walked into the room.

We started with a smudge. A person walked around the circle offering the smoke from smouldering sage as a way for each of us to cleanse our bodies and hearts. Then one of the leaders, whom I had never met before, picked up one of the drums in the centre of the circle and walked toward me. Without fanfare, without words, he simply handed it to me. And when he started drumming and singing, I drummed with him. Our drums beat together, like the pounding heartbeat of Mother Earth that those drums represent. He didn't seem to care that I didn't have great rhythm or that my skin colour was different from his; he simply offered me an opportunity to be part of that heartbeat—a heartbeat that is much bigger than any of us.

Though he didn't owe it to me, this man extended grace and opened my heart to a deeper level of healing. In that moment, I began to see that I could be both worthy *and* wounded, both a representative of the colonizer *and* welcome in the room, both harmed by my own past *and* a co-creator of a vision that moves us beyond the systems that we feel stuck in. It was a full-circle moment, reminding me that the grace I was choosing to extend to those who'd harmed me in the past was also available to me.

IN HIS BOOK *My Grandmother's Hands*, Resmaa Menakem writes about the trauma inherent in colonization and white supremacy. Colonizers from the European continent had trauma in their white bodies, and they spread that trauma around the world.

> During the Middle Ages in Europe, torture, mutilation, and other forms of savagery, particularly on women, were seen as normal aspects of life. Public executions were literally a spectator sport.

As a result, when European "settlers" first came to this country centuries ago, they brought a millennium of inter-generational and historical trauma with them, possibly stored in the cells of their bodies. Today, much of this trauma continues to live on in the bodies of most Americans.

Most white immigrants to the "New World" didn't heal from their trauma. Instead, beginning a little over three centuries ago, the elite among them created the concepts of whiteness, of blackness (and redness and yellowness), and of white-body supremacy which sprung from the seedlings of xenophobic and ethnocentric Greek and Roman empires into plants and trees of race, racism in the British colonies and the supremacy of the white body. The concept of whiteness and of being white is originally a species question not a race question. Are Black peoples human or ape is a species question... The answer to that question ultimately determined who was human and then who was white and who wasn't. Elite white bodies invented and institutionalized the myth that the white body is the supreme standard by which all other bodies' humanity are measured. Then they blew much of their trauma through the bodies of Africans and their descendants—and made lynching into an American spectator sport. This served to embed trauma in Black bodies, but it did nothing to mend the trauma in white ones.

Back in the fourteenth, fifteenth, and sixteenth centuries, my Mennonite ancestors were some of the people on the receiving end of the brutality that was part of European culture. Once, when I visited the Rijksmuseum in Amsterdam, I stood in front of *The Night Watch*, a massive painting by Rembrandt, and tears involuntarily filled my eyes. Dated to 1642, the painting depicts the *schutterij*, civic militia guards who were wealthy citizens of the towns they protected and members of the Dutch

Reformed Church. The people depicted in the painting almost certainly participated in (and perhaps orchestrated) the murder and torture of my ancestors in the Netherlands. Dutch Mennonites were excluded from holding positions in the *schutterij* and charged a double tax in lieu of service. That moment in history marginalized my people from the existing systems of power and sent us a message that we were unworthy.

My people fled for their lives and took their martyrdom and lack of value and agency within systems of power with them. A few centuries later, when they were again facing torture at the hands of the Russians, they fled to North America, taking all those layers of pain and accumulated baggage with them.

When they arrived, Mennonites largely assimilated into what had become the white race in North America. Though they still carried the mark of oppression in their bodies from centuries of brutality, and still held martyrdom as one of their Christian virtues, their white skin allowed them to blend into the dominant culture and acquire power and privilege. Now there were people beneath them on the social hierarchy and they could benefit from this new position. Gradually, more and more Mennonites in Canada and the United States accumulated wealth, became elected officials, and engaged in those aspects of the culture and economic systems that were once out of grasp for them. They participated in the oppression of Indigenous Peoples and others who didn't have white bodies, continuing cycles of harm. Some of the residential schools in our country, where Indigenous children were taken from their homes and forced to abandon their own culture and spirituality, were run by (or supported by) Mennonites. The oppressed became the oppressors.

All this history lives in my body, just as history lives in all our bodies. We have inherited the legacy of both oppressors and the oppressed, and only a few of us can say our lineage lives on only one side of that narrative.

Academic and activist Kimberlé Crenshaw, primarily referring to the complexity of being a Black woman, named this complexity "intersectionality"—that is, "a lens through which you can see where power comes and collides, where it interlocks and intersects." The *Oxford English Dictionary* defines intersectionality as "the interconnected nature of social categorizations such as race, class, and gender, regarded as creating overlapping and interdependent systems of discrimination or disadvantage."

I am a queer woman who happens to be fat, and I have been harmed by the patriarchy. I also come from a lineage of oppression and marginalization on European and Russian soil and have generational trauma in my body from centuries of harm done to my people. At the same time, it is also true that I have white skin and a body that can move in the world without disability. My ancestors became settlers in this country when they were invited by the Canadian government and given land on which to farm. When they landed here, even though they too were placed on "reserves" by the government, they displaced the original peoples of this land, assimilated with the dominant culture, and moved into positions of privilege.

Like the girl in the Velcro dress, I have many layers that I have to peel back in order to understand how each of these identities shapes who I am and informs how I am treated by the dominant culture. I am learning to peel, and I am learning to live at the intersections. Sometimes that's an uneasy existence, sometimes I fumble, and sometimes I am able to see the beauty in all of my complexity.

RECOGNIZING THAT I have certain privileges, I ask myself what it means to be an ally to those who have less access than me to privilege and power within dominant systems. An ally is someone who offers active support for the rights of a minority or marginalized group without being a member of it. But how do I do that without stepping blindly on the toes of the people I'm trying to support? Also, is that enough? Perhaps, as some have said recently, what those marginalized groups need is accomplices rather than allies. Colleen Clemens, in an article on the website Learning for Justice, says: "An ally will mostly engage in activism by standing with an individual or group in a marginalized community. An accomplice will focus more on dismantling the structures that oppress that individual or group—and such work will be directed by the stakeholders in the marginalized group. Simply, ally work focuses on individuals, and accomplice work focuses on the structures of decision-making agency."

As I did when I offered my facilitation skills in service to the conversations about racism in Winnipeg, I have tried for many years, with some fumbling, to be an ally, but I'm still in the early stages of learning what it means to be an accomplice. How can I divest myself enough of the systems in which I receive privilege so that I can work with those more marginalized to dismantle the systems that cause harm and co-create alternatives? That's a question that's alive in me and sometimes I get closer to finding the answer, and sometimes I still feel very far away.

What often keeps me from finding the answer to that question is that I don't always have awareness of what's influencing me, what's still attached to my Velcro clothing. The mix of stories and histories alive in my body means that I sometimes empathize with those at the margins, sometimes slip into "white saviourism" (thinking it's my job to rescue them), and sometimes get defensive when my privilege or mistakes are revealed to me.

The defensiveness is often the trickiest thing to hold in myself, because it's related to those old fears, threaded back to my religion of origin, of being found "sinful" and therefore being cast out of the space of belonging. It's often so quickly triggered that I barely know it's there before I've said or done the wrong thing. Years of learning to be more mindful has helped me hit the pause button and reflect before speaking, but I don't always get it right.

The shadows of martyrdom and codependency also sometimes shape my efforts to be an ally and accomplice. There have been times, for example, when I've taken on too much responsibility for fixing things—or other times when abusive or hateful language came my way because of my privilege, and I accepted it as my responsibility and perhaps even my rightful punishment, subconsciously believing I didn't have a right to boundaries. In my attempts to be a good ally, I have sometimes become a shock absorber for pain, as I did in my marriage and when I was raped, just as my Mennonite foremothers learned to do to survive.

Martyrdom is not allyship, and codependency is not a way to change harmful systems. Martyrdom, even by those with privilege, allows the trauma of oppression to continue through generations and through different groups of people. Similarly, codependency (and the entire Drama Triangle) allows harmful patterns to perpetuate and doesn't challenge anyone in the systems to behave differently.

True transformation happens when the sovereignty of everyone in those systems (communities, partnerships, marriages, or countries) is recognized equally; each person is supported in having healthy boundaries, protection, and support; and there is communal care available for all. That's when we can begin to co-create new systems where, no matter what colour our skin is, what gender we are, what shape our bodies are, what abilities our bodies have or don't have, or what religion we follow, we have access to love, kindness, and grace.

To really make a difference in the systems in which I live, and to become a good ally and accomplice, I've been learning that I first have to believe that I am worthy of love, just as everyone is worthy of love. It's taken me years to unravel the messages that the systems have imprinted onto my body about the value of my body, and a few more years beyond that to learn new patterns for how to treat myself, how to move through the world with grace and love, and how to be in equitable relationships with other people.

As Sonya Renee Taylor teaches, the disruption of harmful systems begins with radical self-love. When I practice radical self-love, I can see not just the beauty and value of my own body, but other bodies as well—and when I truly see that, I stand as an accomplice alongside *any* body being harmed and refuse to accept that harm. Taylor writes, "Radical self-love summons us to be our most expansive selves, knowing that the more unflinchingly powerful we allow ourselves to be, the more unflinchingly powerful others feel capable of being. Our unapologetic embrace of our bodies gives others permission to unapologetically embrace theirs."

AS I'VE grown in my belief that I am worthy of radical self-love, I have discovered that, for me, what it means to be an accomplice is also what it means to be a friend. I want to learn to walk alongside other people, in all of our intersections, with a posture of humility and a willingness to keep learning. I also want to walk with a heart full of love and courage—love that is available for *all* of our bodies and courage that will disrupt and/or divest of systems that harm those bodies. I want to disrupt the game of Barnga until there are no rules that make winners or losers out of any of us and each of us can triumph at the end of the day.

My friend Saleha and I have very different histories, and yet we do our best to stand at the intersections together. Our friendship has been one of the most grace-filled and loving relationships I've ever had, and it has helped heal and reshape me in ways that give me hope for the future. From the moment we met, over a chai latte (me) and strong coffee (her), both of us believed we had found something special. In that first conversation, we quickly discovered that there are surprising similarities between a Mennonite childhood on a farm in Canada and a Muslim childhood on a farm in Saudi Arabia. We were both raised to believe that faith in the divine and an adherence to its laws were important, and that deviation from those laws resulted in God's or Allah's disfavour and punishment. We were taught similar rules about our bodies—be modest, cover up in front of boys, abstain from sex except in marriage, and don't dance or engage in sensual behaviour. Alcohol was forbidden and most popular culture (TV, movies, et cetera) was sinful. Collectivism was valued over individualism, and donations that allowed the church and the mosque to care for vulnerable people were expected. Women were to be submissive to men, and neither of us was granted a voice in church or mosque governance or teaching.

Central to our relationship has been our shared commitment to healing and to understanding the systemic forces that influence us and the intersections we both stand in. We have endless conversations in coffee shops, on park benches, on Zoom, in cars, and on our living room couches about the layers of trauma we're each uncovering and healing. Together we unravel, heal, unravel, heal, and then unravel and heal some more. Sometimes one of us feels more broken and wounded and sometimes the other one does. Always, we hold space for each other for whatever we're going through.

Quite regularly, we discuss the differences that our ethnicities, races, religions, and skin colours make in the ways we view ourselves, the internalized oppression we carry, and the ways we move around in our city, Winnipeg, where whiteness and Christianity are dominant. Neither of us can fully embody the other person's experience, and so we try to help each other understand. As the person with more cultural ease of movement in Canada, I try to understand, notice, and be an ally and accomplice when Saleha is being discriminated against (like when we go to stores or restaurants and the clerks or servers talk to me, the white woman, rather than the brown woman wearing a head covering) without taking her power away.

Recently, we concluded that, while we always want to remain aware of how we're being impacted by our culture, and we want to be conscious of colonization, racism, and white supremacy and the harm those systems do, within the context of our relationship, we want to do our best to consciously co-create something that's set apart from those systems. We don't want to give those systems power or prominence within the relationship, because when we do, we slip into old patterns of pity, power imbalance, martyrdom, over-compensation, and deference. When those patterns show up, we are less able to centre love and equity.

This is not the same as saying "we don't see colour." We do see colour; we see difference in each of us, and we honour those differences. At the same time, we want our relationship to be a small oasis in the world where the differences in colour, religion, ethnicity, et cetera, are not attached to the same meanings they've been given in the culture we live in. We are determined not to use the measurements of value assigned by white supremacy, colonization, or patriarchy.

Together, we choose to disrupt and divest ourselves of the systems that have taught us how to measure ourselves and each other. Within our friendship, after years of examining what influences us individually and collectively, we are determined to be equals and friends, shaking off the burdens and bounds of the systems we're part of and healing our individual and collective trauma. That's the way we believe we can transform what we've inherited and experience shared liberation.

REFLECTION QUESTIONS

INTERSECTIONALITY DESCRIBES the ways that different aspects of a person's identity may expose them to discrimination or confer on them unearned privilege. Until something new has evolved to replace them, we can't live apart from the systems of inequality and can't be fully objective, but we can do our best to at least witness what affects us and others and disrupt the harm being done.

1 How do you identify? (For example, by race, age, gender, sexual identity, disability, body size, socio-economic status, religion, education, and so on.)

2 How do you feel about how you identify? How have those feelings been influenced by your culture? (For example, do you hold any internalized oppression over parts of yourself that are less valued by the culture?)

3 I shared a story of a group playing a game of Barnga, where the man realized he'd been carrying his rules with him. Are there ways in which you do similar things? Perhaps areas where you expect others to experience the world like you do?

4 How do you feel when people talk about privilege? Does it resonate or do you resist it?

5　In which ways are you willing to focus on dismantling structures that oppress, as an accomplice for those who are less privileged by the system?

6　I learned from Sonya Renee Taylor that the disruption of harmful systems begins with radical self-love because that gives us the capacity to also extend radical love to others. Reflect on your own capacity to love yourself and to love others. What might still be getting in the way of your ability to love yourself? What's getting in the way of your ability to love others?

7　What are your intentions for growing your self-love?

8　I believe equitable friendships can disrupt harmful systems and build more just ones. How do your friendships transform you and open you to different possibilities? If you don't yet have such friendships, what can you do to cultivate them?

Power Tools and Paintbrushes

Y HOUSE is breaking in half. Planted in Manitoba gumbo, a clay that shrinks during dry years and wreaks havoc on basements all over the city, the front half of my house is sinking at a faster rate than the back half. Across the middle, there are cracks on opposite sides of the house, in the thick concrete basement walls and in the drywall on the main floor above doorframes and windows. In my living room, beneath the place where the ceiling has a long crack, you can feel the shift underfoot as you walk from the more level ground of the hallway to the sloped ground of the living room. Like a breadstick that's snapped in half by pushing down on one end, it's giving way in the middle.

In moments when victimhood and self-pity are my companions, this feels like a betrayal, as though my house is being deliberately mean to me after the years that I've poured love and kindness into it. Or maybe, if I can anthropomorphize my house enough to lend it feelings, it's the other way around and it's telling me that I am the betrayer. Like a grumpy toddler, it's telling me how unfair it is that I have decided to leave it behind.

I DIDN'T always love my house. In the early days, it started out as love, when we'd moved with our first two children still in diapers, from a tiny house where the main bedroom was so small the bed blocked the door from closing and the only other bedroom was even smaller and barely fit a pair of cribs. This new-to-us house felt expansive then, hopeful and full of expectation. I loved the big picture window in the front. I loved the massive maple trees in front and in back. I loved the quiet backyard with space for a swing set and sandbox. I loved the attached garage that made it easier to leave the house in the cold winter months. I loved the large master bedroom and ensuite bathroom. I loved that there was a grocery store just down the street, a playground across the road, and a river that could be seen from our front door when the water was high. I didn't love the small, cramped kitchen, but I was full of hope that we'd change that someday.

I poured love into the house in the early days, in whatever ways didn't cost a lot of money. I painted the walls, one room after another. I sewed curtains and cushions and reupholstered second-hand furniture. In Nicole and Julie's bedroom, I painted hot air balloons with cartoon characters floating through a clear blue sky. In the living room, I painted a border of golden suns, moons, and stars. When Madeline arrived, a few years later, we moved her into the balloon room and I transformed the third bedroom with bright pink and orange flowers for the older two girls. As all three grew, I updated the painted walls to suit their maturing interests.

Gradually, though, I fell out of love with the house. Slowly, with one disappointment after another, it lost its hopefulness and possibility. The dreamed-of kitchen addition failed to materialize when M quit his job to go to school. The cheerful painted walls started to show wear and tear, and I lost the energy to refresh them. The beige living room carpet, which we'd hoped to replace at the same time as the kitchen renovation, grew increasingly dingy. The backyard, where we'd torn out a rotting deck to make way for the new kitchen and a screened-in verandah, filled up with weeds and we stopped trying to tame them. Thistles and brambles grew where we hadn't bothered to plant grass, and some poked through the sandbox. The swing set started to rust and the children stopped playing on it. Even the furniture seemed to be giving up—couches sagged and kitchen chairs wobbled.

The house mirrored the marriage held within its walls. As I became less and less happy, and less and less hopeful that the wounds we were causing each other would ever be healed, I put less and less care into the house. I stopped inviting people over, and I looked for excuses to travel and be away from home. The clutter increased and, especially in the bedroom I shared with my husband, I stopped putting any effort into making it cozy or even clean. I didn't much want to be in that space and couldn't muster the energy to pretend I did.

WHEN I finally decided to divorce M, I wasn't sure I could afford to keep the house, especially since he was pushing me to pay him out with cash rather than my pension fund, so that he could buy an expensive motorcycle he had his eye on. My business provided barely enough to live on at that point, and self-employment would make it harder for me to qualify for a mortgage. Because I hadn't loved the house for a while by then, I wasn't sure I really wanted to keep it. My daughters needed stability, though, so I applied for a mortgage.

Fortunately, we'd been dealing with the same credit union for many years and had a good credit rating, so they accepted my application, and I bought M out of the house. They even let me add enough money onto the mortgage so that I could do some much-needed repairs.

Even before the land title was transferred into my name, before I had any money for renovations, I started to transform the space back into a home I could love. I wanted to give each of my daughters a safe space where they could do their own healing and grieving during a tumultuous time, so while I was waiting for their dad to move out, I painted and redecorated their bedrooms, letting them choose paint colours and fabric for curtains and cushions. Some of what drove me was the guilt over disrupting their lives, but it felt like the least I could do.

Once their rooms were finished and their dad had moved out of the house, I moved upstairs from the basement family room where I'd slept for several months while he looked for an apartment. First, though, I refreshed the master bedroom, claiming it as my own space, making no accommodations for anyone other than myself. I let him take the bed to his new apartment and bought myself a new one, and then chose art-work and decorations that spoke to me of strong womanhood and liberation.

When the paperwork was nearly finished, and the house was almost mine, I rented a dumpster to take away all the rub-bish that no longer needed to be in the house. I tore out the old flooring, trimmed the overgrown hedges, pulled up weeds, decluttered closets, and tossed anything that wouldn't help our home feel like the sanctuary my girls and I needed it to be. I painted all the walls I hadn't yet touched, and, when the money finally came through and the land title was in my name, I hired a friend to install new flooring.

The last thing I did was thoroughly clean the closet that had been my husband's. Remnants of his presence had been left all over the house, and whatever I'd found, I'd tucked into that closet or the garage. I avoided the final cleanse for quite a while but knew the new beginning I wanted for my daughters and for me wouldn't feel complete until what he'd left behind was out of the house. Finally, when I felt strong enough to face it, I cleaned out the closet, had a good cry (or two), left all his things in a pile in the garage, and told him to pick them up by the weekend or I'd haul them away to goodwill or the garbage dump. Then I scrubbed and painted the walls of the closet and moved in a few of my own things to mark this final space as mine and solely mine.

When everything was finished, and I finally loved my house again, I dipped one of the paintbrushes I'd used in red paint and glued it to a canvas. Beneath the dripping red paint, I collaged the words "Repurpose, Reconfigure, Reimagine" from letters I cut out of a magazine. Like the Velveteen Rabbit, my home, though battered and bruised, had been loved back into realness.

At the front door I hung the following excerpt from a blessing by John O'Donohue:

> May this home be a place of discovery,
> Where the possibilities that sleep
> In the clay of your soul can emerge
> To deepen and refine your vision
> For all that is yet to come to birth.

The following summer, when I could afford to do more, I hired a landscaper to tear everything but my beloved maple trees out of the backyard and put in a brick patio, sod, and a fence. That was the cherry on top of the cake, and my daughters and I soaked every bit of goodness out of that backyard in the summers that followed. Many friends came to sit with us in that backyard, and, in a way, we passed the healing that we benefitted from in the sanctuary of our home on to those who gathered.

THE FIRST TIME I used a power saw on my own was when I had to remove the subfloor in the kitchen. I'd torn out a lot of carpet and linoleum by then, and this was the last job that needed to be done before the new floor could be installed. It felt rather preposterous that I might consider cutting up the flooring myself without anyone guiding me on how to do it, and I thought it likely wise to leave the task for the friend who was coming to install the new flooring, but then the idea that I might be capable of doing it myself started nudging me. M's circular saw (that he'd inherited from his dad) was still in the garage at that point, so I brought it inside, put on safety goggles and leather gloves, and took a selfie to see how it might feel to see myself as a woman who wields power saws.

I have tackled many DIY projects throughout my life, but they had always remained within certain limitations. I'd try almost anything that needed just a little elbow grease and some creativity, but up until that moment, I'd limited my projects to those that held very little risk of me losing a finger. Power saws presented a new level of risk and, quite frankly, they had always been the domain of the men in my life. Now I found myself, as a newly single homeowner, standing at a mental threshold— made up mostly of outdated gender roles and fear—that was inviting me to cross it. And cross it I did. After admiring how badass I looked in the selfie, I figured out how to set the depth of the circular saw and I cut the subfloor, careful not to rip into the floor beneath it. From the very first cut, my body came alive to a new love. I felt powerful and strong, and suddenly capable of so much more than I'd given myself credit for.

A divorce has a shattering quality that I hadn't anticipated. Though I wanted the divorce, and was relieved when it was finally finished, I felt weakened by it, like I'd lost a big portion of my capacity and resilience just when I needed it most. It was a relatively easy divorce, without any dragged-out debates over child custody or finances, but even the easiest divorce isn't truly "easy." To dismantle something I once believed in; to be on opposing sides to someone I'd once assumed would always have my back; to go through endless shame-inducing meetings with lawyers, bankers, financial advisors, and government officials at land title and vital statistics offices; to worry about the well-being of my children; to fret about being able to pay the mortgage or look after all the maintenance needed for solo home ownership; to worry about how people would judge the failure of my marriage—all of it chipped away at my self-esteem, and it felt like a vital part of me had been diminished. Power tools helped me find myself again. They helped me rebuild my faltering self-esteem and reclaim the power I'd given away for so many years in an unhealthy marriage.

After the new flooring was in, I built some simple shelves to attach to the living room wall. Then I increased the level of challenge and built a long narrow table to fit between the couch and the wall. Next, with an inexpensive mitre box and hand saw, I tried my first mitred corners, and built a wooden tray for drinks and snacks.

Each thing I built challenged me a little more than the last. I watched endless YouTube videos, downloaded free building plans, and often fell asleep dreaming of the things I would build next. On Father's Day, when hardware stores held sales that targeted dads, I bought my first new power saw, a beautiful chop saw that can still put a grin on my face. With that chop saw, I built a set of furniture (a sectional couch and coffee table) for the backyard. I sewed bright orange cushions to make it cozy.

Soon my collection of saws and other power tools grew, and I added some to my Christmas list. My daughters laughed at me, but I heard a note of pride in their voices when their friends visited the backyard and they pointed to the furniture and said, "My mom built that."

Before long, the house, garage, and backyard were full of things that I had built—desks, shelving units, cupboards, small tables, a work bench, and a backyard shelter for firewood. Each piece is fairly rudimentary, and there are gaps in places where there shouldn't be, exposed screws, and other marks of an amateur, but every piece is beautiful to me.

The empowerment I felt when I first picked up a power saw spilled over into other things. I learned how to change the blinker light on my car, how to install new light fixtures, how to replace a burned-out switch in the fuse box, and how to replace the bathroom sink and kitchen faucet. Each project increased my self-confidence and put a little spring back in my step. I hoped it was also giving my daughters an increased sense of what is possible for a woman to accomplish.

WHEN I WAS turning the master bedroom into a sanctuary for myself, I didn't yet understand the depths of what I needed to heal in that space. A few years after the divorce, when I was still testing out the language of what had happened and beginning to see that there was abuse, a therapist helped me see just how much my boundaries had been violated throughout the marriage. The bedroom was ground zero for those boundary violations. It's where the two of us were alone and where he felt most justified in pressuring me for sex and pushing past my boundaries. It makes sense, now in retrospect, that I'd let that space become cluttered and uncared for, because that's where I felt the least safe.

When I reclaimed that space for myself, I also started to reclaim my right to safety and consent. It didn't happen all at once, but gradually I let myself be more and more honest about what made me feel unsafe, and I gave myself permission to withdraw from those spaces and relationships where safety seemed illusive and consent was not respected. My therapist coached me in asking for what I needed, and I started to practice it more, starting with my own daughters.

When my children were small, I'd stopped locking the bathroom door because someone always seemed to need me the moment I sat down on the toilet or climbed into the tub. Boundaries don't mix well with babies or toddlers so, like most moms, I adjusted to the idea that I didn't get to have them where my children were concerned. That spilled over into their teen years, and even though I was respectful of their boundaries and, once they were old enough to care for their own spaces, didn't enter their bedrooms without consent, they assumed they didn't have to extend the same respect to me. My bedroom was free range, as was the bathroom attached to my bedroom. Instead of brushing their teeth or washing off their make-up in the family bathroom, my daughters would often burst into my bedroom after I'd fallen asleep and use my bathroom.

After a therapy session, I decided to tell my daughters that I needed better boundaries. Gathering them in the living room, I told them that I was working with my therapist on healing and caring for myself, and one of the things I needed was more respect for my personal space. "I want you to move your tooth-brushes and face cleansers out of my bathroom," I said, "and once I close my bedroom door to go to sleep, please don't enter my room unless something important comes up that needs my attention."

With a bit of a learning curve, my daughters adjusted, and we settled into a new normal where all of us had more permission to communicate the boundaries that felt important to us. Once that felt easier, I expanded that further into friendships.

Especially in those early years, when my healing became my priority, I felt safest with my own space for sleeping, where I could trust that nobody would trigger memories of hands that would grab me when I least wanted them to. After discovering in therapy just how porous my boundaries were, I learned to ask for my own space whenever staying somewhere other than my home. I chose not to share hotel rooms or retreat bedrooms when that was an option, and I took my own small tent along on a canoe trip while most of the women shared a couple of large tents. Old programming told me I was being selfish in those requests, but I pushed through those messages and did it anyway. By then, I had enough self-worth to know that my healing mattered.

At home, my bedroom became my safe space, and I treasured that space at the end of every day. In that space, I wrote in my journal, read books that helped me heal, and worked my way through the grief, fear, and anxiety that had been in that room for so many years. I set up a desk under the window, and since I didn't have a dedicated office space, much of my writing and online teaching happened in that bedroom (especially during the pandemic when my daughters were almost always home).

Surprisingly, though, one of my most significant moments of healing didn't happen in my own bedroom but in one far from home. In Australia, where I have travelled several times to lead retreats and workshops, I usually stayed in the spare bedroom of my friend Georgia, who owned a retreat centre where I have often worked. Georgia is an animal lover whose dogs and cats have the run of the house, and one cat in particular had claimed the bed I was to sleep on. At night, because I am not as fond of pets as Georgia is and didn't want any surprises disturbing me during the night, I slept with the doors firmly closed.

At that retreat, we were talking about safe space and brave space and about how we sometimes need to nudge ourselves out of safety to take a brave step. I'd invited retreat participants to make a collage that represented their safe spaces, and I created a collage alongside them. My collage showed me that my most safe space was, ironically, the space that had once felt the least safe—my bedroom. I marvelled at the fact that I'd managed to transform what had once caused me so much pain.

That night, I went to bed, as usual, with the doors firmly closed. In the middle of the night, though, I woke to discover the cat pushing through the magnetic screen on the window. It climbed onto the bed and curled up between my legs. I sat up, prepared to usher the cat out the door, but then I paused to notice that the cat's entry hadn't triggered my body into the usual fight, flight, or freeze. Even though the cat had, rather ironically, climbed through my window just as the man who raped me had done years before, I wasn't agitated by its presence. Instead of pushing it away, I settled into a comfortable sleep, with a cat purring between my legs.

The next morning, I shared my story with Georgia and the retreat participants and said, "Maybe I don't need my safe spaces as much as I once did. Maybe I'm ready to take a brave step and let others into the spaces I've guarded so carefully."

That night I slept with the door slightly ajar, less concerned about the interruption of cats or dogs, trusting that their presence would be healing rather than harmful.

EARLY IN the pandemic, and then each time a new wave brought more lockdowns, I would have minor panic attacks when thinking about spending too much time in my house. By then, I'd learned to love the space again, but I wasn't sure I could stand being in it all day, every day, together with my three daughters, especially when I couldn't travel anymore or even work in coffee shops or public libraries.

I've dealt with mild claustrophobia at several stages of my life and these house-bound panic attacks felt a little like that. It didn't help that my version of the hot flashes that many women suffer from during menopause showed up as claustrophobic flashes, prompting me to sometimes rush out of theatres, tents, or other closed-in or over-stimulating spaces, or to get panicky on airplanes when stuck in a window seat at the back of the plane.

The walls of my house seemed to be closing in on me, and there weren't many other spaces I could go. Even grocery stores in those early days felt like unfriendly foreign landscapes with their social distancing arrows on the floor.

Sometime between the third and fourth wave, though, I turned the corner and no longer felt panicky about spending so much time stuck in my house, despite the fact that the second pandemic winter was settling in, and my options were even more limited. Instead of feeling panicked over being stuck inside, the opposite was true, and I had less desire to be anywhere but home. Perhaps it helped that I was nearing the end of menopause, or perhaps it was simply about accepting the uncertainty and lack of control that the pandemic brought.

When the restrictions started to lift, I finally had the opportunity to leave the country and fly to Costa Rica, where Mary had invited me to stay at her home while I worked on this book. As the time drew near, I wasn't as excited as I normally am in advance of travelling. I had learned to love being home in a way that I'd never loved it before.

PERHAPS YOU are wondering why, after pouring so much love into my home and finally becoming more of a homebody who feels safe in her home, I am preparing to sell my house and move elsewhere. There are moments when I wonder the same thing.

I think it's because I've received all the gifts that this house has to offer me, and it's time to embrace whatever's next. This house helped me raise my daughters and grieve my son; it held me when I got the devastating news that my dad had died suddenly in a farming accident; it soothed me after I watched my mom die of cancer; it supported me through my husband's suicide attempts and then my divorce; it offered me space to heal and learn to love myself again; it gave me a canvas on which to paint new dreams; it let me practice skills that empowered me; it let me transform its rooms and close its doors so that my body could learn to feel safe; it gave me a space to write books and build a business.

I don't yet know what's next. I don't know if I'll ever own a home again. I don't know which city or even which country I'll choose to settle in. I don't know if I'll stay single or find a partner with whom I want to create a home. I don't know if I'll settle somewhere as soon as I sell the house, or if I'll buy a van and travel around North America for a while. Or perhaps I'll live part of the year in one place and part of the year in another. With daughters all landing in different cities, parents now dead, and friends spread all over the globe, I have little attachment to any particular place and no reason to stay where I am.

Sometimes these limitless possibilities feel exciting, and sometimes they scare me. Sometimes I am tempted to change my mind, close the door, and return to my place of safety. But while safety is good for healing, it's not good for growth, and I know that it's time for me to do some more growing. I will set out from this safe space and make a brave step into whatever's next, just as Georgia's cat showed me I could.

Perhaps, if I can anthropomorphize my beloved house one more time, the cracks are not revealing a betrayal. Perhaps they are an invitation. Maybe the house is saying, "You can go now. You no longer need the safety you've worked hard to create within our walls. You can dare to open your heart and let it expand into the next place that's ready to hold you. You have our blessing, now go."

REFLECTION QUESTIONS

WE ARE SHAPED by the people we live with and the places where we live. As you reflect on your own relationship with "home," I welcome you to consider whatever that word conjures.

1 What is your relationship with your home? How might you like to change that relationship?

2 What relationships have you had with homes in the past? How have you been shaped by the places you've lived?

3 How might you claim a space for yourself to support whatever journey you're on?

4 When I renovated my home, I hung a John O'Donohue blessing in the entryway. Write or choose a blessing for your home.

5 For me, power tools became a form of empowerment and a symbol of healing. What practice or skill might you adopt that would similarly empower and heal you?

6 How might your home become a sanctuary for your healing? What boundaries are needed for it to feel safe for you?

7 What next move (a physical move or a symbolic one) would support your journey now?

8

The Value of a Home

THE PROCESS of selling my house started with a bang when a real estate agent saw me naked. It was 8:30 a.m., and I was emerging from my bathroom, where I'd been blow-drying my hair, into my bedroom, where I was about to get dressed. He was standing there, in my hallway, looking completely flummoxed. And then he disappeared.

My real estate agent (not the one standing in the hallway), had told me that the first viewing by a potential buyer was happening at 9 a.m., and I'd planned to be dressed and gone from the premises before then. Because of some mix-up, this other agent had booked an 8:30 a.m. showing that hadn't been communicated to me.

I dressed quickly and hurried out of the house. At the doorway, I saw a large pair of men's dress shoes, an unusual sight in a house that had housed only women for the past seven years. Outside, in my driveway, stood the young, flustered agent, in his socks. I suppressed a giggle when I considered the mad dash he'd made from the house. Trying to save face (but not looking at mine), he swore to me he'd booked the appointment and swore he'd called out when he'd let himself into the house. I brushed it off, climbed into my car, and drove away.

Throughout the remainder of the day, as I juggled the chaos of running a home-based business amidst multiple showings, I burst out laughing whenever I remembered the man in my driveway without his shoes.

Only later—perhaps the next day—did I surprise myself with the realization that the encounter did not trigger me. A strange man intruded on my private space and saw me naked, and . . . I laughed! It felt even more significant than the cat in Australia.

OVER THE next few days, my sense of humour had dwindled. The chaos of having my life so frequently disrupted started to take its toll. Though no other agents saw me naked, they wanted to come at all hours of the day, they changed their appointments at the last minute, and I was left juggling the many Zoom calls my work requires with expectations that I be out of the house so that people could snoop through my bedrooms and poke around in my kitchen. Ten minutes before teaching a class, after learning of a last-minute scheduling change, I rushed to my sister's house to borrow her internet and kitchen table.

The agent's gaze on my naked body affected me less than the parade of people whose gaze was falling on my naked house. I didn't know what to make of that. Despite my efforts to distract myself, including a short road trip out of town with my sister-in-law over the weekend, when the greatest number of showings was happening, I couldn't ignore the churning in my stomach when I thought of all those people in my private space, looking through my closets, intruding on the sanctuary of my lovely backyard, possibly judging my stained furniture, and casting a critical eye on the cracks in the walls and peeling paint on the kitchen cupboards.

There were moments when I wanted nothing more than to chase them all away, change the locks on the doors, and hunker down in my own house, protecting it from intruders. There were moments when I wanted to yank the For Sale sign out of the front lawn and commit to the house that I would never, ever leave it.

A WEEK after the naked encounter with the agent, the date arrived when my agent would accept offers. There had been about thirty showings in a week, so she expected a bidding war that would land far above the asking price. It didn't turn out that way. The repairs needed on the foundation, the cracked basement walls, and cracked living room ceiling had scared people off more than we expected. We'd priced it much lower than comparable homes in the neighbourhood, knowing that it would require repairs, but even that low price didn't convince people it would be a good investment. Add to that a recent interest rate increase and talk of a recession, and buyers had become more reluctant than they were a month earlier.

The only offer I received was below the asking price, and there were conditions that included a full inspection. I declined the offer and countered. They declined that with another counter-offer, just a bit higher than the first. I was heartbroken about how low the offer was, but I gave in, knowing that there was very little chance anything better would surface.

I SPENT a lot of time crying in the next few days as I waited for the house inspection to happen and the deal to be final-ized. I cried about people not loving my home as much as I loved it, about the twenty-nine people who looked and then turned away, and about all the work I'd put into the house in the last seven years that now felt like a financial waste. I cried because I would leave this home less financially stable than I'd hoped to be at the beginning of the next phase of my life—and because it's surprisingly easy to turn "they don't value my house" into "they don't value me."

Especially on the day that the house inspection happened, I cried. For three hours, I had to be away from the house while a stranger poked even deeper than all the people who'd come before. This time, they would evaluate every square inch of the house, critiquing the windows, the furnace, the appliances, the walls, and the foundation. This time, they would open every closet and look for leaks under every sink.

I woke up that morning suddenly remembering that there were some old mildew stains I hadn't cleaned off the trap door at the top of my closet that opens into the attic. It was one of the only spots I'd forgotten to clean in the two-month frenzy to prepare the house for sale. I worried that the inspector would take the mildew too seriously and warn the buyers to back away from the deal. I covered the clothes hanging in my closet with an old blanket, climbed onto a chair, sprayed bleach onto the ceiling and scrubbed.

A few hours later, when it was nearly time for the inspection to be over and for me to be allowed back in, my agent called. The inspector wanted to know if he could move the clothes in my closet to access the trap door into the attic. I said yes, both relieved that I'd taken the time to clean the mildew stains and annoyed to know that someone was currently rummaging in my closet.

When I got home, there were far too many signs that someone had been in my house and the frustration boiled into rage. I felt disrespected and somewhat violated when I saw how many items had been moved away from walls and not returned to their rightful places. On one of the hottest days of the year, all the curtains had been pulled open and the furnace had been left on.

AS I PROCESSED the grief, shame, and disappointment that the sale and home inspection were bringing up in me, I considered that perhaps some of those feelings were older than my relationship with my house. Perhaps I was also carrying some of what had always been unresolved in my mom.

Just as she carried body shame throughout her life, my mom carried house shame. I remember her, when I was seven, feeling so excited and proud that we could finally build a house and move out of the tiny green two-room shack we called home. I remember her disappointment when nobody liked the colour of the dark stain she'd chosen for the wooden trim. I remember the shame she felt when anyone dropped in and the house was a mess. I remember how often it was my job to clean up the manure my dad's farm boots inevitably left on the basement stairs on Saturday night, in case anyone came for lunch after church the next day.

And then there was the time, after I'd moved away, when a portion of the living room ceiling caved in because of a leaking roof. For several years, my parents lived with that gaping hole, the attic insulation sagging through it. For years, Mom made embarrassed apologies when guests stepped into the living room.

When Mom and Dad were moving out of the house and I was pregnant with my first child, I stood and watched, with mixed feelings, as my dad finally repaired the hole in the ceiling. I felt admiration when I discovered he was actually good at the craftsmanship required, but pain and regret when I considered how long Mom had waited for him to fix it and how long she'd lived with the shame.

Just as I know it's not my fault that my house is sinking and the foundation is cracked, my mom knew it wasn't her fault that the roof leaked. But that knowledge didn't stop either of us from feeling the shame that seemed to be programmed into our bodies.

WHAT IS the value of a home? As I waited through the evening for my agent to give me the final word, I asked myself that question. Can the value of this home, that has held so many of my heartaches and borne witness to so many of my wounds, really be measured by a dollar figure on the piece of paper my agent passes across the table to me? Can any amount of money tell of the worthiness of this house, when it has been a refuge through so many storms?

It's what we've learned from capitalism, I realized: that worth can and should be measured. We've been taught to commodify our lives, our bodies, our stories, our talents, our land, and all our possessions, placing the value of one above another, diminishing it all to a dollar sign on a piece of paper. This belief is so tightly attached to our Velcro clothing that we are blind to any other way of witnessing the world or ourselves in the world.

Feminist rage boiled up in me as I realized the grief and shame that I'd been feeling about people devaluing my home was the same old grief and shame I'd felt about people devaluing my body. "The basement is cracked and the house is showing its age," they'd said, casually, as if the measure of a home could be commodified. "Take $50,000 off its value."

"Your body is fat, female, and showing its age," they'd said, casually, as if my body could be commodified. "Knock a few points off its value."

My agent finally arrived, and the evening dragged on with multiple back-and-forth phone calls while the buyer's agent pointed out what the inspector had revealed. He tried repeatedly to bring the price down even more. Fed up, I said a firm "No" when my agent was on the phone with him. "He heard your no," she said when the call ended, and I wasn't sure if she was admonishing me or cheering me on for being so clear. Either way, I didn't regret it. I knew that I had the power to walk away rather than let this agent chip away any more of what had value, and I would carry my head high, whatever the outcome.

Finally, the sale went through, and my agent left. I crawled into bed exhausted and sad.

THE NEXT MORNING, it began to settle in that I had sold my house. The remnants of grief still clung to me, but I became resolved to pick myself up and carry on. "It's only money," I told myself. "It says nothing about the value of my home and even less about the value of me."

I looked around my home and saw it through the eyes of love. I peered out my bedroom window and watched the birds land in the branches of my sturdy maple tree and the squirrels scamper across my fence. I touched the walls with tenderness, like I used to touch my children's skin when they were little. I softened my gaze as I peered at my naked body in the mirror. Home and body—both priceless, both worthy, both loved.

I remembered the words of Sonya Renee Taylor about how the world expects "a certain set of apologies to already live on our tongues." I felt that in my body and I felt it in my home. Standing there, looking in the mirror, I shook off that apology.

"Think of body shame like the layers of an onion," Taylor writes. "For decades in our own lives and for centuries in civilization, we have been taught to judge and shame our bodies and to consequently judge and shame others. Getting to our inherent state of radical self-love means peeling away those ancient, toxic messages about bodies. It is like returning the world's ugliest shame sweater back to the store where it was purchased and coming out wearing nothing but a birthday suit of radical self-love."

The only way to disrupt a system that oppresses people by measuring their worthiness is to stop complying and stop measuring.

A FEW WEEKS after a strange man saw me naked in my bedroom, I noticed a shift in how I thought about the people who had passed through my house since then, measuring the worth of what I love. I was finally able to laugh at them, too. I could picture them all in my mind's eye—prospective buyers, agents, and inspectors—lined up in their socks in my driveway, unable to look me in the eye as I walked by. In that picture, my head is held high, and I am dressed not in a shame sweater, but in my birthday suit of radical self-love.

How much could that young real estate agent know about the value of an aging, fat, saggy female body? He knows nothing of what this body has carried, how this body has triumphed, and how many times this body has nurtured and protected those who are scared or lonely. If there is shame to be had in that moment when this body was seen naked—and I'm not suggesting there is—then it is not mine to carry.

Similarly, nobody who walked through those rooms can know anything about the value of my home. They could peer into the closets and peek into the attic, but nothing they could see with their untrained eyes would tell them of the stories my house has held or the way it has sheltered my family through the storms.

If there is shame to be had in the cracked walls or mildew stains, I refuse to carry it. When I walk away from this home that I have loved so dearly, ready to start the next chapter in my story, I will do so with my head held high. There may be fewer dollars in my bank account, but the value of what this house has given me will never be measured by that.

REFLECTION QUESTIONS

IN THIS CHAPTER, I discover how the messages around my home's value were intertwined with the messages around my body's value. This chapter is also about how capitalism has taught us to measure worth and apply that to our own bodies and each other's bodies. Consider the parallels in your life—the ways in which the value of what you love has been diminished and whether it feels like your own value has been diminished, too.

1 How do you value your own body? What messages have you received about it?

2 How do you measure the worth of other people's bodies? Are there some unconscious biases about which bodies have more (or the most) worth?

3 What shame might you be carrying about your body? How can you "get naked" as a way to liberate yourself of that shame?

4 Write a letter to your body. Express how you feel about it, and then do your best to express gratitude to it for all that it has done and carried.

5 What does liberation feel like in your body? What might it look like for you to walk in the world with a liberated body (instead of a shame sweater)?

6 What is your vision of a post-capitalist world?

9

A Time to Hold and
a Time to Let Go

RIVING HOME from the hospital with a brand-new baby, after a painful and exhausting week that involved many complications related to the birth, I was struck by the enormity of what had suddenly been entrusted to me. I was a mom. The life of this tiny new being was in my hands. I wasn't sure I had the right skills or knowledge to keep her alive. I had a poor track record for keeping houseplants alive. How would I manage with a baby? "Maybe you're driving too fast?" I said to my then-husband, who was driving no more than the speed limit.

Nobody taught me how to parent, just as nobody taught my mother before me how to parent. The only modelling I'd had for parenting was from my own parents, and I know now that they were muddling their way through just as every parent does. (They didn't even have the benefit of the myriad books or blogs now dedicated to parenting.) Growing up, we didn't live close to aunts and uncles, so there weren't many models to contrast Mom and Dad's parenting style with. I just assumed it was the way parenting was done.

Nicole and Julie were born in quick succession (sixteen months apart), and what I remember most from those days is exhaustion. I had six months of maternity leave from my government job for each of the first two, and then went back to work and juggled a full-time management-level job along with full-time motherhood. To minimize their time in daycare, M worked the late shift, so it meant that he was the solo parent in the morning and I was the solo parent in the evenings. Somehow, we muddled through, and, at the very least, we kept them alive.

If you'd asked me, back then, about what I wanted for my daughters, I would have said, "I want them to be whoever they choose to be. I want them to learn to be true to themselves." I knew enough about the ways I'd felt limited in my life to want more freedom for them. I wanted them to be able to make more liberated choices and to worry less about what others thought of them.

MY DAUGHTERS' favourite game was the Game of Life. I grew tired of it and found it rather cringe-worthy that it centres capitalism as the driving force in a person's life, so I often tried to convince them to choose something else, but they kept insisting it was The Best Game Ever. Again and again, they played it, roping in any adult who would humour them.

In the game, a player starts out on the road of life alone, choosing either the pink or blue figurine to represent them as the driver of their car and then choosing to either go to university or skip it and get a lower-paying job. Along the way, the player adds a spouse and children, gets a job, and accumulates a home and wealth. The player with the most wealth at the end wins. The rules are always the same—get married, have babies, make money, accumulate things, win at life.

Though my daughters liked the game, they almost always tried to subvert it, sometimes choosing the least lucrative career or the most run-down house. Every time we played, Nicole insisted on choosing a same-sex partner and resisted adding children to her car.

While those choices were perfectly okay when I was playing alone with my daughters, they always caused me some internal conflict when my mom or other family members were present. "Maybe you could choose a husband instead of a wife when Grandma's playing with you," I said, afraid of the judgment that might come. "Why?" Nicole asked. "I thought you said I can love whoever I want to love." "Yes," I said, painfully aware of the mixed messages I was sending, "but Grandma's still kind of old-fashioned that way and she might not like it."

It hurts me, now, to think of the ways that I taught my daughters to hide who they were so that they could receive love that felt conditional, but I was still hungry for my mother's love and approval and wanted them to have it, too. There was a part of me that still believed the only way I could get that love was to pretend to live the way my mom wanted me to live. Parenting well-behaved children who didn't disrupt the Game of Life was one of the ways I tried to pretend.

Several years later, after my mom died, Nicole came out of the closet and assured me she had never changed her mind about not wanting children. She did an art project for her degree in fine arts about how much it hurt her that her grandma, who loved her very much, never got to see her in all her realness. If I could go back, I'd let her drive proudly across that board game with a female partner and no babies in the car, the way she always knew would fit her best.

IT WAS the birth of my stillborn son, Matthew, that most awakened in me a desire for greater liberation. In a sense, he helped me disrupt my own Game of Life. Before that, I'd been on the path most guaranteed to bring success in the game, driving along in my little plastic car with my heterosexual marriage and two children, buying a house, getting a good government job, and accumulating at least a pension plan if not wealth. It was the path I believed I was meant to take and, even though I wasn't truly happy with it, the game had taught me to believe that happiness was just around the corner.

Suddenly, there was an obstacle along the path. An unexpected pregnancy that I wasn't sure I wanted landed me in the hospital. The surgery meant to close my prematurely opened cervix failed. Then all I could do, under the supervision of medical professionals who monitored my baby carefully through twice-daily ultrasounds (mostly to see if he was peeing regularly), was wait and hope that my baby would survive. I couldn't go to work and I couldn't look after my two daughters. My employees had to take on increased responsibility in my absence, and Nicole and Julie went to the farm to stay with my parents.

In those three weeks between the failed surgery and the stillbirth, my journal was my constant companion. In that journal, I started to re-evaluate my life. Was I truly happy? Was I satisfied with the way life was unfolding? Was I simply going to accept the default path in the Game of Life, or was I willing to disrupt it and choose differently?

Though I didn't have the language for it at the time, my hospital stay was when I first discovered that I loved to hold space for people as they worked through struggle and examined their life choices. People seemed to gravitate toward my room— friends, family, nurses, doctors, and other patients—and many shared with me something they were struggling with. I would listen and then ask questions that helped them consider a new perspective. Almost all of them told me that it made a difference.

When I emerged from the hospital after three weeks, with full breasts and empty arms, I knew that my life's path had been altered by Matthew's short life. I was no longer willing to accept the default path. I had to look for more meaning, purpose, and liberation. A few years after that, I did what I'd seen my daughters do when they chose to subvert the Game of Life. I quit my government job, took a pay cut, and started work in a non-profit international development agency. When I took that job, I committed to myself that it would be a temporary step toward fulfilling a larger dream of being self-employed. Six and a half years later, I started my own business and pursued writing, teaching, and coaching as full-time work.

My daughters were feeling anxious about me quitting a good-paying job, and I worried that with diminished finances I wouldn't be able to give them everything they'd grown accustomed to, but I also believed that the risk would ultimately be worth it for me as well as for them. I wanted to show them that they didn't need to stay stuck in work that made them unhappy. I wanted them to see that they could take chances and find ways to do work they were passionate about.

Fortunately, the risk paid off for all of us, and after a few years of fumbling, my work grew enough to support the family even through the divorce that eventually came. The Game of Life was successfully disrupted.

AT AGE TEN, Madeline was the first of us to come out. "I'm bisexual," she said to all of us (me, her dad, and her two older sisters). "I've known for a couple of years already."

And then... not much happened. There was no major drama. Nobody fussed over her. Nobody cried or laughed or did anything dramatic or monumental. We simply told her, "Cool. We love you. Thanks for telling us." And then we went to a restaurant as we'd already planned to do that evening. It wasn't much different from when we discovered she was left-handed. We just kept on teasing her the same way, loving her the same way, and nagging her the same way for not doing the dishes.

Nothing changed, really, and that was a strangely beautiful thing.

I wept after she came out—not in front of her, but behind closed doors. I didn't weep because I was disappointed in her or worried about her; I wept because I was just so very happy that she was *safe*—to speak her truth, to reveal herself in this way at the tender age of ten, to assume she wouldn't be teased or shamed by her immediate family for this aspect of her identity that made her different from many of her friends.

I wept because we'd managed to create, in our children's home, what I'd always longed to have in mine, a circle of grace where, as much as possible, those in the circle didn't feel judged or shamed and everyone could be themselves. Despite the ways I still carried internalized shame and wasn't confident about how my extended family would treat someone in the family who wasn't heterosexual, at least in our small family, we'd helped her feel safe.

A couple of years later, the tears welled up in me again, in the back of a concert venue full of mostly queer teenagers. We'd driven to Minneapolis so that Madeline could attend a Troye Sivan concert. Troye is an openly gay musician who has a large queer following. Standing around the edges with the other parents as our children danced and sang along to every word, tears welled up in my eyes because our kids had such a space where they could feel safe and accepted. I didn't yet know that some of those tears were because I needed that myself.

Later, Madeline told us she's a lesbian rather than bisexual. And still nothing changed. We kept loving her. And then her oldest sister came out, and her middle sister, and finally... me. Yes, we are a queer family—lots and lots of queerness. We toss around terms like "bisexual," "lesbian," "non-binary," "gender fluid," and others. And, to be honest, I'm not entirely sure which label each embraces right now, but we're clear on one thing—we are each free to love who we want to love and use whichever pronouns fit us best. That kind of liberation makes me very, very happy. We create a safe space for each other and also for our friends who don't always feel safe in their own homes. Once more, the Game of Life is disrupted.

FOR ALL my fear about how much the divorce might harm our children, I can say now, in retrospect, that hanging on to the marriage too long did more harm than the divorce. Mistakes were certainly made in the divorce, but it did not destroy the girls. When we told them their dad was moving out, Nicole's first response was, "It's about time!" Julie soon communicated something similar, once she recognized how much more peaceful our home had become after the marriage ended. It was hardest on Madeline, who was thirteen and continues to be the most attached to her dad, but even she has since seen how it was the best choice for all involved.

There were many sleepless nights, before and after the divorce, when I didn't know how to support my daughters through this disruptive time in their lives. I offered to pay for therapy, and they have all since taken me up on that offer, finding therapists who helped them talk about the things that are hard to say to one's mom. I sought my own therapy and we learned to talk about mental health just as we talk about gender and sexuality, as casually as one might discuss the weather or one's favourite bands.

Just as nobody teaches you how to parent, nobody teaches you how to help your children get through their parents' divorce.

I muddled through, as best I could, and tried to take responsibility and apologize whenever I made mistakes. Slowly, we built a new family unit, strengthening the bonds that had sometimes been wobbly in the past and learning to be honest with each other when the hurt felt bigger than we could bear alone.

The hardest part was facing some of the regrets from my marriage, like the fact that my daughters hadn't always felt protected, especially as teenagers. I am grateful to them for the courage they showed in bringing that to me and in being willing to work through it together so that I could do better in the future. As I learned more about showing up for them in ways that helped them feel safer and more protected, I also learned to do the same for myself. It turns out that, while sacrificing my own safety for my daughters, I hadn't really been keeping anyone safe, and I certainly wasn't teaching them how to prioritize their own needs.

THE PANDEMIC came at a challenging time for my daughters, when each was set to launch into adult life in their own unique way (Madeline graduating from high school, Julie starting the honours year of her psychology degree, and Nicole graduating with a fine arts degree in the early days of the pandemic), and I am sad for the things they lost during that time, but there are ways in which I will always be grateful for that time when we all hunkered down and focused on keeping each other safe. We learned new things about the value of personal and collective safety, especially since we needed to be extra careful to avoid exposing Madeline, who is immune-compromised, to the virus.

At first, when schools and workplaces started to shut down and my daughters were spending more time at home and had to cancel plans to travel and to move out of my house, I was anxious about how we'd get along and if we'd all grow tired of one another. But we settled into this new normal and I began to appreciate the fact that I got a bonus year to deepen the relationships with my girls before they started moving away from home.

YOU COME home from the hospital with a completely dependent baby in your arms, and from that day forward, parenting is an exercise in learning to let go. With each development, the baby becomes more independent and takes a step away from you. One day they're learning to use a spoon without your help and the next day they're going away for a sleepover at a friend's house.

In 2021, I had to learn new lessons in letting my daughters go. The year prior, whenever I considered that two of my daughters were planning to move out at the same time (one to Toronto and one to Vancouver, cities more than two thousand kilometres away in opposite directions from Winnipeg), I'd find myself dissolving into minor panic attacks. My throat would close, my brain would start to buzz, and suddenly I'd be gasping for air and fighting tears. And then I'd soothe myself by slipping into denial, because... really... could this *actually* happen, especially during a pandemic when we'd all become so accustomed to hunkering down and barely leaving the house? My mamaheart did everything it could to shield me from the thoughts my mama-brain was trying to have about this sudden upcoming transition from too-full nest to nearly empty nest. "Nope," I'd tell myself. "It likely won't happen. The fourth wave will come, their universities will shut down, or... maybe one of them will change their mind?"

Then August 2021 arrived, and suddenly it was time for them to start packing for the move. A week before I was set to leave for the first trip to deliver Nicole to her new school (where she intended to add a jewellery design degree to her fine arts degree), I wrenched my back so badly I could hardly move. For a week, I was in so much pain, I didn't know how I'd sit in a car for the three-day drive to Toronto, help Nicole move her belongings up two flights of stairs, and then make the trip back home again. I tried everything I could to resolve it—physiotherapy, chiropractor, massage, acupuncture.

By the time we were set to leave, the pain was more manageable. I drove with the sticky-pads of a TENS machine attached to my back as my physiotherapist suggested, flicking the switch to send little electrical jolts into my muscles when the pain flared up. By the time we were in Toronto, my back was strong enough that I could carry boxes up to her third-floor room.

I spent four days in Toronto getting used to the idea that I would leave Nicole behind in the middle of this big busy city, and she would begin a life without me nearby. She'd learn to navigate this city on her own, and when I came back to visit, my status as "well-travelled expert/mom" would have diminished, and she would know these streets better than I would.

We made multiple trips to Walmart and IKEA until her small room was fully stocked with the things that would be harder to attain when she no longer had access to a car. I watched her decide on cleaning products and bedsheets, and sometimes she'd turn to ask my opinion. I paused before giving it, wondering whether this was a moment when she needed a mom's expertise or if she needed to choose for herself. I gave opinions tentatively, knowing whatever she bought would all belong in a home that was not mine to manage or care for. Mostly, I just provided the transportation and furniture assembly skills.

One evening while I was still in Toronto, we both had a moment when the immensity of it hit, and neither of us could find meaningful expression for how that felt. As introverts, we both knew, without saying it out loud, that we each needed space after those intense days together. I drove to the beach, walked on the sand, and put my feet in the water. She crawled into her new bed under her new blanket and napped. Later, I brought her a carton of greasy poutine and we curled up together to watch *Twilight*, a movie that reminded us both of simpler times when she was a teenager and living in the safety of my home with her sisters.

A few days later, in a hotel room on the long drive home, after a FaceTime call with Nicole, I melted down under the weight of all my sadness. My friend, who'd flown to Toronto to make the drive back with me, sat with me as I cried. She didn't say much. She, too, had left a daughter behind in Toronto, a few years earlier, so she knew this was simply a moment I had to pass through.

I worried about who would hold space for Nicole when she cried, in a city where she knew no one. For twenty-five years, for almost all of her meltdown moments, I had been her person.

A WEEK after arriving home, I was ready to set out again, this time heading west, to Vancouver, where I would leave Madeline on campus at the University of British Columbia. We packed the car one more time, and this time Julie came with us. She would be the only one returning home with me.

In B.C., we passed places where forest fires were still burning, and we watched helicopters dropping water from the sky. The grief of a burning world threatened to consume me, but I pushed the thought away, knowing I only had enough capacity to hold the grief that was right in front of me. I worried for Madeline, though, so primed to pay attention to the grief and fear of climate change that she'd become a climate activist two years earlier. How would she be able to hold all that as she dove deeper into environmental studies? She joked that her time at university would be short because the planet would be destroyed soon, but under her sardonic humour I knew there was pain.

In Vancouver, I made the same trips to Walmart and IKEA for bedsheets and cleaning products, and it felt like déjà vu. Once again, I tried to withhold my opinions until they were requested. Once again, I listened to the complaints about how annoying it was to buy toilet paper just to flush it down the drain. Nicole sent texts from Toronto to the family chat about the annoyance of paying to do laundry, and my daughters commiserated with each other about the frustrations and expenses of becoming adults. I chuckled but resisted saying, "Do you see how much I've done for you all these years?"

While they complained and joked, I marvelled at their adaptability. I watched them each do things I didn't know they'd become capable of. The tension in my neck and chest began to relax as I tried to reassure myself that I'd done all that I could to help them prepare for adulthood and they would get by without me. And yet... a part of me still stressed about the things I should have taught them when they were under my roof. Did I miss some critical parts of their education? Would they bump up against things that might surprise them because I forgot to warn them?

When the morning of our departure arrived, I wondered, for the second time, about how much emotion I should reveal and how much I should hold back to release when I was alone later. Should I let my daughters know how empty the house would feel, or should I focus on the fact that I'd be fine, and would soon find ways to fill the empty spaces in my life and home? Would my tears let them know how much they are valued, or make them feel guilty for leaving me behind? If, however, I was too stoic, would they think they didn't matter to me?

I remembered how my own mother's grief had sometimes become my burden. When my siblings and I grew up and left home, her loneliness became our guilt. Nearly every time we spoke with her, she expressed how much she wished we'd call her more often and how she was afraid her life no longer mattered to anyone. Determined not to let that family pattern pass on to the next generation and not to attach more things to their Velcro clothing, I tried to ensure my daughters that they had my unconditional support in these big, brave moves.

Before Julie and I left, Madeline joked that now would be the time for me to say something toxic, to try to coerce her into coming home. "No," I said. "I will not be responsible for you changing your mind about something you want. I don't want to be the person you blame in therapy ten years from now for ruining your life." She turned to Julie, who was feeling the grief as much as I was, and said, "How about you? Do you want to say something toxic?" Julie's response was similar to mine. As much as we wanted her home with us, we wanted her to follow her dreams more.

We said goodbye and we all cried.

IT WAS HARD to leave my baby in Vancouver, but it was especially hard after the eighteen months we'd just had together. A month before the pandemic hit, she was diagnosed with a rare disease (idiopathic subglottic stenosis) that keeps closing her trachea and making it hard for her to breathe. Since then, she's had surgery each time her trachea closes. Nine times I'd taken her to the hospital for surgery, and for seven of those trips, when the pandemic rules changed things and she had, by that time, turned eighteen, I had to leave her at the front door of the hospital. I couldn't stay with her as her advocate in the health-care system, and I couldn't be at her bedside when she woke up from surgery. Two of those times, while I was at home waiting, I got a call from the surgeon saying that her oxygen levels had dropped suddenly after surgery, and they'd had to revive her from near death.

About a year after the diagnosis, after she switched specialists because the first one wasn't very proactive, she was referred to a third specialist and received a second tentative diagnosis for a rare and scary auto-immune disorder (granulomatosis with polyangiitis) that was likely at the root of the problem with her trachea and could possibly cause other serious problems in her body. They started treating her with immune-suppressing meds with a long list of side effects. A team of specialists began working on her behalf. Meanwhile, we lived with the anxiety that there was a deadly virus lurking just outside our door that could be especially deadly for her. We were all extra careful not to expose ourselves, lest we expose her, and we all got vaccinated as quickly as we could.

Now here I was, after months of that kind of vigilance, about to leave her behind, in a new city, where she'd need to meet with new specialists and learn to navigate a whole new healthcare system. Alone. When I thought of the enormity of that, I was filled with both panic and admiration. This was a brave thing my girl was choosing to do. I assured her I would be available for conference calls with specialists and could fly to Vancouver for surgeries, but that was the best I could do. This was part of letting go that nobody warned me about when I held a tiny, dependent baby in my arms.

BEFORE SETTING OFF for home, Julie and I took a ferry to Victoria for a short holiday. On a whim, because we were both feeling sad and wanted to do something nice for ourselves, we splurged on a whale-watching tour. The Zodiac zoomed over the waves toward the open ocean and I decided, even before we saw whales, that this was the perfect way to release some of the big emotions bottled up inside me. Just like in Toronto, when I went to the beach, I had found my way to water. In the fast-moving boat, with water splashing all around us, nobody could tell my tears from salt-spray.

We found a pod of killer whales and our skipper told us what he knew about them. It was a family of four, two males and two females, who'd been together for many years. Experts' best guess is that this pod is three generations of whales—a grandmother, a mother, and two sons (though the females may also be sisters). The oldest female is believed to have been born before 1955 and the second before 1965. That means that the two females have been together since the year before I was born. The sons were likely born in 1995 and 2001, around the time I was having babies.

I marvelled at this family that had stayed together all these years, and my longing made me envious. I had never wanted to be a killer whale, gathering the generations around me into a pod, before that moment.

We left the whales behind before I was ready to say goodbye. When we were back on the dock, the skipper pulled me aside to offer us a free trip the next time we came, because there were noisy kids on the boat and he worried that they were rather distracting when we should have been able to watch the whales in silence. (Perhaps he'd noticed my tears after all.) I wasn't bothered by the chatter, but I accepted his offer, promising myself I'd be back the next year to spend more time with the whales.

Maybe the mama-whales could teach me what it means to swim wild in big waters and still hold your family close. Maybe they could teach me how to use echolocation to reach through the water for my faraway daughters.

ON THE WAY back through the mountains, we were stopped on the highway by a construction truck. The sign on the side of the road said that blasting was taking place up ahead. Julie and I sat in our melancholic silence and waited for the boom. On top of the cliff ahead of us, there was a large black object that looked like machinery. When the blast came, the black object flew into the air and revealed that it wasn't machinery after all. It was a stack of blankets made of thick black rubber that contained the blast and prevented the rubble from hurting anyone or spilling over the road. A few minutes later, the construction vehicle moved, and we were allowed to pass.

As a mother grieving the distance from my daughters, I felt like that blast site, trying to put rubber blankets on my big emotions so that the rubble wouldn't harm anyone close to me. I made a mental note to gather the blankets I might need in the coming weeks.

BACK HOME, I wandered around the house feeling lost and untethered. I began to turn Nicole's empty bedroom into an office for myself and I cried as I did so. Some moments I was fine and looked forward to the spaciousness that would now be mine, and some moments I dissolved into a puddle of tears.

I felt more ungrounded than I'd felt since early adulthood when I moved away from my parents' home. With Julie set to leave at any moment herself, I no longer needed to provide a home for anyone other than me. With no partner, no living parents, and no in-laws, I was not tethered to any family commitments and didn't need to provide care for anyone who was aging. With a portable business, I could work from anywhere and didn't need to stay in any one place. I was tethered to neither place nor people, neither work nor obligations. Nobody expected me to put their needs at the centre of my plans anymore.

There might be a time when this would feel like freedom, but that time hadn't arrived when I stood in Nicole's former bedroom and painted the walls. At that moment, everything still felt liminal.

TEN DAYS after we got home, Julie went for long-anticipated (and oft-delayed, because of the pandemic) elective surgery. It seemed routine and there was little risk, but my body remembered the stress of the past year, and my body also knew, because I had birthed a stillborn son, that children can die. While she was in surgery, I found it impossible to focus on anything else. I went for a long drive and stood by the river, just as I'd done in so many liminal moments before this one. Some of the grief came out and because there was nobody around who might get hurt by the rubble from the blast, I didn't bother with the rubber blankets.

It took too long to hear from her after she should have been out of surgery, and I couldn't relax until I knew she was breathing and alive. I called the clinic and was told she was fine. When I picked her up, I wanted to wrap my arms around her and tell her she could never leave me, but I resisted.

Now, six months later, I am in Costa Rica writing this section of the book while Julie makes her first solo trip, backpacking around Mexico. While she prepared for the trip, a couple of weeks ago, I was already away and limited in how much I could support this big adventure she was about to embark on. Once again, I had to loosen my grip and let go, trusting that yet another daughter had the skills she needed to navigate the world without me close by.

Before she left, Julie texted the group chat, to me and her sisters, "Soon, we will be in three separate countries, with thousands of kilometres between us and nobody in our house. Mom, you sure have raised adventurous daughters!" Yes, indeed, it seems I have. None of them has chosen the most acceptable path on the Game of Life, and none is trying to win by the game's rules.

I LEARNED RECENTLY, after writing the first version of this chapter, that there's an updated version of the Game of Life. The peg people are now pink, blue, red, purple, yellow, and green; and players can choose any of them. The definition of "family" has expanded and players can now add pets and friends to their cars. Players can also choose whether or not to get married, and marriage costs money and time rather than adding value to their bank accounts. Children are also optional (and not guaranteed) and can be in a player's car whether or not they choose the marriage path.

On the social media post where I learned about these changes, a conservative Christian mom who homeschools her children referred it as the "dystopian Game of Life." She concluded her post with "Wokeness ruins everything."

If I ever have grandchildren who want to play the Game of Life with me (and I have no expectation that I will be a grandmother, since only one of my daughters has shown interest in becoming a mom), I will happily watch as they choose whatever path, family, or peg person they wish, and then I'll encourage them to disrupt the ending and choose another definition of success that's not attached to a bank account.

To the homeschooling mom, I would say, "Do you know how liberating it is to finally wake up?"

REFLECTION QUESTIONS

WHEN I TEACH people about what it means to hold space, I often say that parenthood was my PhD program in the subject. At the beginning, I had to hold space tightly, protecting my children and making sure their needs were met. As they grew more and more independent, though, I had to learn to gradually let go and recognize that they are sovereign individuals with lives separate from mine. Whether or not you are a parent, I expect that there are ways in which this chapter might resonate with your own relationships and how you've learned to walk alongside others without clinging too tightly.

1   Which of the rules in the Game of Life have you learned to disrupt, and which still need to be disrupted?

2   I encouraged Nicole to choose a blue peg for a partner when she played the game with my mom, a choice I later regretted. In what ways have you made similar choices to be found acceptable by your parents, family, caregivers, friends, and so on?

3   What moments in your life have awakened you to a need for more meaning, purpose, and liberation? What did they open up for you?

4   If you're a parent or caregiver, in which moments in your children's lives did you feel most afraid, when you had the least control? What did you learn from those moments?

5   What choice might you be afraid to make because of the effect it will have on other people?

6   If you were to re-create the Game of Life, what would you add or subtract? Alternatively, imagine a new game that reflects your vision of life.

10

Becoming Tender

"YOUR BODY'S energy feels quite guarded, like you're protecting yourself from something," a massage therapist once told me, a few years ago when I was nearing burnout from my work and knew I needed to take better care of myself. To put it frankly, her assessment pissed me off because I was doing a lot of work (writing and hosting retreats) that involved considerable vulnerability on my part and I often felt like I was overly *un*guarded, allowing too many people access to me. I wasn't sure how much more unguarded I could be.

It took a long time for me to understand the wisdom of what she'd offered. It was true that I was giving a lot of myself away, in my writing and teaching work, in ways that felt vulnerable and generous. It was also true that my nervous system was almost always at least somewhat guarded against real or perceived threats. Every time I'd put something vulnerable into the world, as I do regularly on my blog and social media and in workshops, I'd brace for attack. Share, brace, share, brace—that had become the nature of my work and life. Sometimes I was tempted to shut it down completely and go back to traditional employment, but by then the work had become so important to me and felt so much like a calling that I wasn't willing to stop.

Instead of running away, I had to change how I showed up. Firstly, I had to learn better boundaries, and secondly, I had to find the kind of healing that would help my body feel like she didn't have to brace for attack all the time. I started taking longer periods of time away from the work and entrusting more of the work to my business partner and our team. When I took breaks from work, I'd stay off social media entirely, since that was often the space where I felt most vulnerable to attack. Whenever I was triggered, I'd turn to the practices that soothed me—journal writing, walking, somatic therapy, havening touch, or Epsom salt baths.

Those practices were helping, but they weren't helping enough. I needed something deeper that wouldn't just give me tools to deal with the temporary flooding of my nervous system but would help me heal the longer-term guardedness that was in my body from so many years of trauma overload (what's often referred to as c-PTSD, complex post-traumatic stress disorder).

When things got particularly bad and I found myself in a conflict that escalated because I reacted poorly during a triggering situation, I started therapy again. That's when I discovered how old some of the trauma in my body was, like the constriction in my throat that I wrote about in the chapter about my rape. It's also when I admitted to myself how much trauma had been impacting my relationships throughout my entire life. The massage therapist wasn't wrong about the guardedness—I'd been resisting intimacy because of what it triggered in my body.

After a few months of regular therapy sessions, on a day when I told my therapist I didn't have much to talk about because life was going well, I found myself talking, once again, of my body's distrust of joy. I told him about how I'd spent a lovely afternoon wandering alone on a nearly deserted beach, and how I'd started the drive home feeling blissful, but suddenly my mind started needlessly ruminating over an old conflict that had been disruptive to a relationship. I could think of nothing that brought the old conflict back to the surface, since I hadn't thought about it in quite some time and there was no reason to think about it now, but there it was, disturbing my contentment. I asked my therapist to help me explore why I couldn't stay in the blissful feeling I'd had at the beach and why my brain tried to sabotage my contentment.

"Do you trust the joy?" he asked.

"I don't think I do," I said. "It makes me feel too vulnerable, like someone will take it away from me. I think I sabotage it so that I have control over the loss of it. And maybe I punish myself for having joy because I don't believe I'm truly worthy of it."

"What could you have done, in that moment when the spiralling started, to return to the peace you felt at the beach?" he asked. "Is there a way for you to communicate to your body that it is still safe, that nobody will cause you harm when you are joyful?"

At this point, I was standing. My therapy sessions (which happen via Zoom) always involve some somatic exercises as my therapist helps me pay careful attention to what my body needs. As I stood there, I closed my eyes and tried to imagine what would have helped my body as I drove back from the beach. I started to sway and the motion reminded me of the waves at the beach. "I think I can bring back the feeling of the waves," I said. "In the waves, I have learned to feel safe and happy, even when I am not fully grounded. I can choose to bring my body back there, even when I'm not physically there." I realized, as I stood there, that my breath was flowing like the waves, just as my body was, in and out, in and out, advance and recede, advance and recede. Breath could be the portal that would bring my body back to the beach. Breath could remind me that I was both liminal and grounded. Breath could bring Tenderness into my body.

A FEW WEEKS LATER, on the anniversary of the day my mom died, the following words flowed onto my journal page, almost without conscious thought.

I am sitting with Tenderness this morning.
Tenderness filled my teacup with green tea,
steeped to just the right amount of strength,
and then she added honey for the sweetness.
Tenderness invited me to sit near the window,
where the sun shines in.

"You need the vitamin D," she said. "And the warmth."
Tenderness gently reminds me what today is—
the anniversary of the day I became an orphan.
(Tenderness knows even adults become orphans
when they lose their mothers.)
She lets me feel all of the feelings I need to feel
and she expects nothing in return.

Tenderness invites me to bring my journal
to my seat by the window, to linger a little longer
before I start my work.
She knows I need extra time this morning,
and she's spent many years teaching me
to guard spaces on my calendar for times like these.

Tenderness was there with me, two days ago,
when a beloved friend
told me that he's dying.
She held my hand when I committed to that friend
that I'd be on the hard and holy journey with him,
no matter how much it hurts.

She was also there with me, a few days before that,
when another dear friend told me
about the layers of pain she's unravelling
as she prepares to free herself of a story that
has long kept her chained to shame that shouldn't
    be hers to hold.

And she was there on Sunday night
when I couldn't be in the emergency room
with my faraway daughter,
and had to sit
and wait for news.
Tenderness knows a lot about mother love.

Tenderness reminds me that these stories—
dying moms, dying friends, wounded friends,
    sick daughters—
need slowness, spaciousness,
and hearts that have enough room to be open.
She knows they need green tea with honey
and a leather-bound journal with a favourite pen.

Tenderness doesn't give two hoots for productivity.
She's not fond of timelines or to-do lists.
She has a habit of pulling me away from computer screens
and sending me into the woods
or under the thick blanket made by my mother's hands
from the wool of my father's sheep.

I don't know exactly where Tenderness came from, but I know that she showed up exactly when I needed her, when I was ready to treat myself differently. Right from the start, she was mostly external to me, as though it were too big a step for me to imagine that she was a part of me. It was easier to receive the love offered to me by this practice if I didn't have to feel responsible for initiating or channelling that love.

Earlier that year, after reading the book *Discovering the Inner Mother* by Bethany Webster, I'd started a new journal practice to nurture all the parts of me that were connected to old stories, and to learn to mother myself better. Each morning, I would sit down with my journal (often on the dock in the local park, one of my favourite summertime journal-writing spots), and I'd write a question at the top of the page. "Which Heather wants to show up on the page today?" And then I'd wait a moment to see which voice from my past wanted to be heard.

Sometimes it was the preteen who wanted to tell me about how she felt like an outsider at school because she grew up Mennonite and didn't have a TV, never got to read *Teen Beat*, didn't have any entry points into the celebrity-focused conversations loved by her classmates, and got shamed for touching her friend's naked body. Plus, her family was poor and she wore hand-me-down clothes.

Sometimes it was the young mom who wanted to speak about how overwhelmed she felt, with babies and a demanding job, and how she doubted herself and wished she had more of a community to lean on, especially when her husband struggled with mental illness.

Whoever showed up, I held space for her, as a patient and loving mother would, and when she'd finished speaking, I'd assure her that she was safe, protected, and loved and that I would always listen to her and make choices that held her best interests at heart.

After doing that for a while, I realized that there was something missing from my journal practice. I was allowing the voices of Wounded Heather to show up on the page, at whatever age she was, but I hadn't yet invited Playful Heather, Passionate Heather, or Sensuous Heather onto the page. I hadn't yet considered that Wounded Heather might have silenced some voices because expressing those other things didn't feel safe, like the young girl in that bed with her friend who already knew what her body wanted. It was the same pattern of distrusting joy that I later discussed with my therapist.

I started listening to the voices that had been silenced. I invited Sensuous Heather to tell me what she most longed for. I asked Playful Heather what her favourite pastimes were. I let Passionate Heather guide me in seeing the world through her eyes. I asked those voices to tell me when they were silenced and what I could do to set them free.

When I sat with my journal on the anniversary of my mom's death, that practice of mothering myself suddenly became a Practice of Tenderness. My inner mother now had a name, and she was ready to lovingly care for me, protect me, and help me feel safe.

SOON, I was having regular conversations in my journal with Tenderness. And then I started imagining living in a house that Tenderness built for me...

"I've built a house for you," Tenderness said, and then she threw the door wide open. "All parts of you are welcome."

I watched as she gathered my parts into her beautiful space.

The infant, torn first from the womb and then from the arms as her mother lay bleeding nearly to death. The little girl who learned about hell and was afraid she might be sent there some day. The preteen who internalized shame and banished desire. The teenager who cried alone when nobody seemed to see the world the way she did. The college student who was ashamed of her body and afraid nobody would ever want to touch her. The young woman who cowered in her bed while her rapist threatened to kill her. The new bride who quickly learned to soothe others and put her needs last. The lonely young mom who didn't have a roadmap for parenting and didn't know who to confide in. The young wife whose husband tried to kill himself. And then the older wife whose husband tried again. The labouring mom who knew her baby was about to be born dead. The daughter whose dad died suddenly in a farming accident. And then the older daughter who watched her mother's final shuddering breath. The writer who struggled to have her voice heard. And then the entrepreneur who risked it all to follow her dream. The woman who finally stopped struggling to save her marriage and let it go. The single mom who supported her daughters through illness, therapy, and healing. The seasoned woman who finally chose to put her needs and desires at the centre.

Each of those parts of me, and more, filed in the door as Tenderness held it open.

They settled into the comfortable furniture, relieved to finally find their way home.

I marvelled to see them all there, together, finally.

No longer in exile. No longer alone.

Tenderness was teaching me to love them all again.

THIS NEW Practice of Tenderness changed my relationship with myself. It helped me find radical self-love. It helped me strengthen my boundaries, hold space for my emotions, honour my longings, embrace joy, and, most importantly, stop abandoning myself.

"I think it's time to stop gaslighting yourself," Tenderness said. "Whenever you do that, you send parts of yourself into exile."

"What do you mean?" I asked, genuinely puzzled.

"You often downplay the pain that you've experienced in the past, you tell yourself not to take things so seriously, or you internalize a challenging situation and assume it must be your own fault."

"But... I don't understand what this has to do with sending parts of myself into exile."

"When you do that, you silence the part of you that is feeling pain, betrayal, disappointment, or anger. You tell that part that those feelings aren't valid and that you're not willing to hold space for them."

"I've never thought of it like that before."

"Remember yesterday, when your friend asked you about that hard time when your daughter was in the hospital, and you brushed it off and didn't admit how afraid you were?"

"Yes. I guess I felt vulnerable admitting how scary it was."

"I understand that, but what about the part of you who lived through it and needs to be witnessed? What about *her* feelings? You're pretending she was fine, and in the meantime, you're brushing her aside, ignoring her many complicated emotions."

"I guess that's true. I never thought of it that way before."

"Imagine if a member of your family told you about their pain, disappointment, or fear, and you said those feelings weren't welcome in your house, that they had to either shut them down or leave. That's what you're doing to yourself on a regular basis."

"I don't know what to say... I guess I've been cruel to myself."

"Dear one, it's what you knew how to do. It's what you'd seen modelled and it's what you were taught in childhood. You were just trying to survive. I'm not telling you this now so that you'll criticize yourself for doing it. I'm telling you so that you can welcome those parts back."

"How do I do that?"

"Listen to them. Let them tell you how they felt. Believe them. Bring them back into the circle of your heart. Witness the full range of their emotional experiences if they feel the need to express them."

"Some of them are pretty deeply hidden by now. It might take a while."

"I know. They probably won't trust you to keep them safe, at first. Remember what you've learned from having a mindfulness practice. Notice, label, be curious, let pass. You're not going to cling to those emotions. They don't control you. And you can take the time that's needed with them so they don't overwhelm you. That's what this house was built for."

ONCE I WAS ready for it, Tenderness helped me write this book...

Tenderness tapped on my bedroom door. "Come in," I said.

"I just wanted to check in on you," she said. "I noticed you pulled out your memory box today."

"Yes, I revisited some of my old journals for my writing project."

"How was that? Did some emotions show up to join you?"

"Well, at first, it was mostly Nostalgia and Comfort, as I pulled out my tiny baby shoes and that doll blanket my grandma made for me. But it got harder when I got to the layer of the box where my journals were."

"Lots of older parts of you are tucked away in those journals."

"Yes, I usually avoid them because they bring up too much pain. Grief, Fear, Frustration, and Anger were living in those old journals and I don't always know how to hold that for the younger parts of me."

"Were you feeling more ready for it now?"

"Mostly. Therapy has helped. And living in this house that you built for me helps. I can see now how some of those parts have felt abandoned because I haven't always been truthful about the pain they carried. So I invited Courage and Love to join me as I held space for those parts."

"What did you learn about yourself as you did it?"

"When I was visiting the parts of me that survived my twenties, I really heard the longing and loneliness in her voice. And one of the things that came through strongly was how she never really had an ally, champion, or protector she could count on."

"She was experiencing all those big things and nobody stood up for her, protected her, or kept her safe?"

"Right. Some people tried, but they didn't always know how to help her feel safe. She tried so hard to fulfill her dream of becoming a writer, but no one opened doors for her or championed her writing. And when she got hurt, she couldn't find a place where she felt safe and protected. She figured out how to survive on her own, she became guarded, and she let go of some of her dreams."

"So . . . some of your resilience is a way of coping with trauma and covering up your real needs and desires?"

"Yes, I think so."

"It sounds like she needed a safe haven and secure base but didn't have those things so it was hard for her to thrive."

"That's right. She was a courageous young woman, and people always told her how brave and strong she was, but that was the only way she knew how to survive. She didn't have, and didn't know how to ask for, a place where she felt unconditionally held. She didn't know how to access Tenderness back then."

"I'm sorry. That must have been hard. And how does it feel to witness all this now?"

"Well, at first I felt resentful on her behalf, but Resentment and I had a conversation and I realized she was just doing her part to mask those deeper feelings that I didn't know how to hold space for back then—Abandonment, Fear, Insecurity, and Grief."

"And you gave those feelings space to express themselves without getting too attached to them?"

"Yes . . . just the way you've taught me to do." As I spoke, Pride snuck into the room and sat on the bed next to me. I didn't chase her away.

"Do you see what you're doing right now?" Tenderness asked.

"No, tell me."

"You're giving that young woman what she needed and didn't know how to ask for. You're providing that safe haven and secure base. You're re-mothering yourself."

"I didn't think of it that way before, but you're right."

"And do you feel stronger now, and more able to hold space for those big emotions?

"Yes! I do! I feel like I can be my own ally and champion. And I have you, Tenderness, and this house you built."

"Yes, and you always will. I'm sorry nobody taught you how to access me back in those days when you needed me. But I'm glad I'm here now."

REFLECTION QUESTIONS

IF YOU'D TOLD ME a dozen years ago that tenderness would become one of my superpowers, I wouldn't have believed you. At that point, I believed that tenderness was the equivalent of weakness, and so I did my best to deny that part of myself. I wanted to have a thick skin, to be seen as competent (and therefore unemotional), and to be tough and resilient. It wasn't until I'd unravelled that story and let go of the beliefs around it that I realized that tenderness was not only the path to healing and liberation, but it was also strength.

1 How do you feel about tenderness? Is it something you embrace or something you push aside? (Reflect on tenderness in yourself and tenderness in other people.)

2 What boundaries might be needed for your tenderness to reveal itself?

3 With the help of my therapist, I discovered my distrust of joy. What emotions do you distrust?

4 In the development of my tenderness practice, I found it easier to consider Tenderness as an entity outside of myself. Imagine you can spend some time with Tenderness. Write the conversation you'd have.

5 Write a letter to your younger self in the voice of a loving parent.

6 My tenderness practice helped me recognize the ways in which I was gaslighting myself. In what ways might you be doing the same?

7 Write a list of the younger versions of you that need tenderness.

11

What My Dad Taught Me

AT A family constellations workshop, I once watched a woman unravel the chains that kept her tied to her father. She loved her dad dearly but acknowledged that she struggled with unhealthy patterns from their relationship, even years after his death. Her dad spent time in prison when she was young, and, according to her childhood memory of that time, it was because he hadn't kept all the receipts for his business. She'd since become irrationally afraid of throwing paperwork away.

In constellation work, the facilitator invites a client to identify people in the group to serve as stand-ins for each of the people or groups in a person's narrative, and sometimes for an inanimate part of the story, like the challenge itself. (In my constellation at that workshop, for example, when I was wrestling with the completion of my first book, someone stood in as my book.) In this case, with the facilitator's guidance, the woman chose someone to represent her dad, someone to represent her, and someone to represent the papers she couldn't throw away.

At one point, the woman started to cry. She realized that the reason she'd hung on to so many pieces of paper was because she wanted, desperately, to hang on to her dad's love. The little child who still lived within her did everything she could to keep her daddy close.

When her tears had settled, the facilitator turned to her and said, "I notice something that I'd like to ask you about. Are you aware of the similarity in the clothing that you and all the people you chose are wearing? You all have shirts with stripes on them. Do you think perhaps it's because you're keeping yourself in jail, as an over-association with your dad?"

The woman looked dumbfounded, but she nodded.

Then the facilitator turned toward the person standing in as her father. "Is there something you'd like to say to her?" she asked.

"I want her to be free," the dad stand-in said. "I don't want her to be behind bars like I was."

By then, most of us in the room had tears in our eyes. An hour later, at lunch, the woman went home to change her shirt. She came back wearing sunny yellow.

THAT STORY wasn't about me, but several years later, I realized it could have been. My dad never went to jail, and I don't cling to paperwork, but, much like that woman, there are things I hang on to because the little girl in me still wants to cling to her daddy's love.

One of the things I've clung to most stubbornly is a belief my dad passed down to me: that struggle is a path to godliness. In other words, to attain righteousness, one must be engaged in struggle. One does not have worth unless life is hard.

I wish I could say that this was only a "head" belief that I could challenge in myself and it would simply go away, but it goes much deeper than that. It is a fully embodied belief, to the point that if I am not engaged in the struggle, my nervous system gets activated, and I start to feel anxious and hypervigilant.

After the house was sold and I was packing my belongings into a storage unit and getting ready to head off on a months-long adventure, I finally started to identify and then unravel the strings that attached me to this belief. I had a few months in which to do all the packing and dismantling of my life in Winnipeg. I was doing it gradually and didn't need to rush. I had approximately seven to-do lists going on at once and was well on track to get everything done in time. It was a surprisingly peaceful and slow-paced process. I had enough spaciousness to have morning bike rides, journal-writing sessions, long conversations with friends, and even some afternoon naps.

Some part of my brain, however, was not convinced that I was on track, and my nervous system agreed. A part of me kept insisting that I was going to forget a lot of things, make bad decisions, and drop lots of metaphorical balls if I didn't maintain a constant state of hypervigilance. My brain and nervous system would make up problems just to make sure I had something to worry about and something to stay busy with.

·On one of my morning bike rides to the park, where I was regularly spending time with my journal, I suddenly realized that I was inventing struggle and I knew exactly why. There was a little girl in me who clung to the struggle because it made her feel safe and loved. Just like the woman keeping all her papers to stay connected with her dad, the little girl in me was insistent that, in the absence of struggle, she was unworthy of her dad's love.

GROWING UP on the farm, pleasure never came before struggle. On the extremely rare occasions when we planned a fun family outing (to the beach or a family gathering), we'd start getting ready for the event (and even sometimes be in the car, waiting) only for some crisis on the farm to derail everything. My dad would have to deal with the crisis (and, more often than not, we'd have to help him), and the fun event would evaporate in the mist. Sometimes it was a broken water pump, sometimes a cow in labour, sometimes a leaking roof, or sometimes a dead car battery. We got to be known, among our extended family on both sides, as "the family that shows up late and only if nothing is going wrong on the farm."

The message for us was that always, *always*, the farm, the work, and the struggle took priority over pleasure. If we ever finally got to the pleasure part, it was because we'd somehow managed to earn our way there.

Christmas mornings were torturous. We'd wake up with the anticipation of presents, but then we'd have to wait an excruciatingly long time before they were available to us. First, all the farm chores had to be done—the pigs, cows, and chickens fed and watered—and then we had to go to church. Usually, while at church, we'd listen to all the other kids brag about the presents they'd already opened, and we could contribute nothing to the conversation because ours remained unopened. It was only late in the afternoon that we'd gather around the tree, and then—as though we hadn't waited long enough—we'd have to listen to Dad read the Christmas story from the Bible, then we'd sing a few Christmas carols, and *then*, finally, we could open our presents.

It was the same when it came to entertainment. Anything for the sake of pleasure was questionable and permitted only after the work was done, if it was allowed at all. Once, when I was a teenager, my older brother (who lived away from home by then) brought home a TV and VCR for the weekend (since we had neither in the house). On Sunday afternoon, my brothers, sister, mom, and I were all in the living room watching *Throw*

Momma from the Train when suddenly the TV died. Dad had flipped a breaker in the basement, cutting the power. He'd come in from the barn, poked his head in the living room, saw that we were laughing at something frivolous instead of helping him with the chores, and decided to end our fun.

The priorities were clear: work and struggle first, religion second (or perhaps tied for first), and then, somewhere near the bottom of the list, pleasure.

SEVERAL YEARS AGO, trying to understand my dad better, I wrote this poem.

Father

I know a man
who fights the Prairie
like a Kamikaze warrior

Death at the hands of the enemy
is the shortest distance to God

He writes his anger
in furrows of blood
and chants his lament
in trenches of pain

The Prairie laughs
as it tortures him
with bullets of hail
and red blades of fire

He comes so close to God

(I hated you
that spring

you made me fight it with you
Rising from our beds
to drag half-dead cattle
from icy water
to watch them die
on higher ground)

I know a man
who caresses the Prairie
like a Shakespearean lover

Death in the arms of a mistress
is the shortest distance to ecstasy

He writes his poetry
in long sonnets
of barley and hay
and sings his songs
in wheatfields of gold

The Prairie laughs
as it kisses him
with tender raindrops
and purple rays at sunset

He comes so close to ecstasy

(I loved you
that summer
you let me caress it with you
Sitting on your lap
on that old John Deere
your large hand
over my small one
as we plowed black soil
and planted the seed)

I contemplated showing it to my dad at the time, but never worked up the nerve, unsure of whether he'd feel insulted or seen.

A few years after I wrote it, Dad died "in the arms of his mistress" as the poem foretold. He was baling in the ditch beside the highway, and for reasons we can't fully know, he stopped his tractor on a slope and walked behind the baler (perhaps to look for a flat spot to drop the bale). Unsurprisingly, because he always had faulty farm equipment that he couldn't afford to fix, the tractor no longer had an emergency brake. When he was behind the baler, it rolled backwards, and he was crushed. A couple who was passing by on the highway stopped and asked if he was all right. He tried to get up, said, in his understated way, "No, I don't think so," and then passed out and bled to death from a deep gash on his back.

Dad died $700 short of being debt free. That discovery, a week after he died, when I was helping my mom sort through the finances, broke my heart. I wish, for once in his adult life, that he had discovered what it felt like to owe no person, bank, or corporation anything. I wish he had known at least that much liberation from the struggle.

I WISH I could say that recognizing this connection between struggle, worthiness, and my dad's (and God's) love is enough for me to heal it, release it, and live differently, but it's more complicated than that. Regularly, whenever my life feels too easy and/or I am not producing something or contributing to the struggle in some way, I feel my nervous system activate and I start punishing myself for being unproductive or worthless. I'm learning to lean into the discomfort of that and inquire into it with mindfulness, but often, instead of allowing myself the pleasure or ease, I find busy-work to do, or I numb the restless sensation with food or social media.

I'm writing this chapter in Sitges, Spain, a month into my nomadic adventure after selling my house. I'm in a third-floor apartment with a balcony overlooking the beach, in a delightful historic town that has seemingly endless quaint streets to wander down, and seventeen beaches stretched out before me along the Mediterranean Sea. The weather has been perfect, and every day there is a new delight happening right outside my balcony, from parades to wine festivals to musical performances to sporting events. This place is *made* for pleasure. It's also one of the most queer-friendly places in Europe, and the beaches and restaurants here feel safe and welcoming for *all* bodies and *all* kinds of love. I love it here. It's a good place to rest and play after the intensity of moving out of my house.

And yet...

I am struggling to fully embrace the pleasure and to feel safe in embracing it. I'm having endless wrestling matches in my brain: part of me wants to be outside soaking in all the things this city has to offer and part of me keeps insisting that I need to get some work done to earn it. The most necessary work was completed last week, and there is no particular deadline to get this manuscript to the publisher (though they are eager to receive it), but just like when I was packing up my house, I am inventing struggle, telling myself I have to finish writing this chapter before I go to the beach. Or I have to prepare for my upcoming workshops. Or I have to write a social media post to promote my training programs. Surely there must be *some* struggle in order to be worthy of this much goodness. The little girl in me is certain of it, and she's convinced my nervous system it must be true.

One of the things that happens nearly every afternoon, directly in front of my balcony, is that a bubble artist comes to create ethereal bubbles with a couple of sticks and some string. It's a marvel to watch him. Sometimes there are hundreds of bubbles at once and sometimes just a few large bubbles that morph and wobble as they make their way toward the sky. Almost always, the bubbles float directly toward me and a few of them make it over the balcony railing and land inches from where I sit. I can't help but pause and get caught up in the magic of them when I notice the bubbles float past my peripheral vision. It's almost like the bubble man is whispering to me, "Don't you think it's time to come out and play?"

I wonder about the bubble artist. Is he confident that this daily act of art-making is meaningful and worthy? Does he know that he's creating magic for people who need it in their lives? Is he Zen-like and fully present as he does his dance with his sticks and strings to make glistening pockets of air that disappear in an instant? I hope so. I hope his body fully inhabits his art and that he has no doubt of its (and his) value. I hope he doesn't spend his days trying to convince himself of his worthiness. I hope he never hears his father's voice in his head, trying to convince him that he is not worthy unless he is producing something that lasts longer than a bubble.

I want to be more like the bubble man. I want to make art that doesn't need to be measured by its permanence or its contribution to the struggle. I want to stand on a beach and watch bubbles disappear into thin air.

I'm going outside now and I'm going to drop some euros into the bubble man's cup. I want him to eat for another day so he can make bubbles again tomorrow.

MY DAD was not two dimensional—like all of us, he contained multitudes. He taught me about struggle, but I would be remiss if I didn't say that he also taught me about delight.

Dad knew how to find beauty in small things. His favourite flower was the dandelion. He believed it to be underappreciated and undervalued, and so he bestowed some value on it by loving it. Sometimes, when he came home from the field, he would bring my mom a bouquet of wildflowers that always included dandelions. He delighted in newborn piglets, calves, ducklings, and chickens, and sometimes he would come into the house and insist that we come outside to see something newly born on the farm or he would bring it inside for us to see. He had a twinkle in his eye and a great sense of humour, and I miss the way his eyes would light up when I'd walk into the room.

I wonder, sometimes, about the internal conflict that my dad carried. As I tried to express in the above poem, I witnessed in him some wrestling, between the struggle that he believed to be the path to God and the beauty that he intuitively knew to be the path to God. Did he consciously believe he couldn't have one without the other? Or was he, like I have been for so many years, endlessly, subconsciously, trying to prove his own worthiness to his own parents, and to his God?

I like to believe that, now that he has been released from his earthly body, my dad has found a release from his struggle. As my friend Randy believed about his own death, I want to believe that Dad was released into "pure joy," and that his soul has finally healed whatever conditioning caused so much of his life to be wrapped up in struggle. I also want to believe that, if he can see me, he smiles when he witnesses me choosing to live differently than he did, trusting that my healing has been worth it. I choose to believe that Dad is now a champion for my joy.

REFLECTION QUESTIONS

IN HIS BOOK *The Myth of Normal*, Gabor Maté talks about how our personalities are made up of all the ways that we learned to survive and make sense of the world in our childhoods. That resonated with me, because there are parts of my personality that were shaped by what I learned from my dad. It's taken a lot of time to unravel that, and I continue to ask myself, "Who might I be now, without that belief?"

1   Reflect on the way your parents or caregivers lived. What did you see in them?

2   What beliefs or behaviours might you have adopted from witnessing the way your parents or caregivers lived? How and why might you still feel attached to those beliefs or behaviours?

3   Do those beliefs hold true for the way you want to live your life now? If not, what do you need to do to release them?

4   I realized I was hanging on to what I learned from my dad because, even after he died, there was a little child in me still wanting to prove she was worthy of his love. In what ways does this resonate for you? Whose love might your inner child be seeking?

5   In what ways might you re-parent yourself so that your inner child can receive unconditional love?

6   The healing work I've done for my inner child has allowed me to let go of disappointment over what my parents were unable to give me and recognize that they were doing the best they could. In what ways might you still be holding a similar disappointment? What might help you release it?

7   What are the beautiful things you picked up from your parents or caregivers?

12

Embracing Joy

A FEW YEARS AGO, at a writing retreat I was facilitating in Australia, a participant approached me and asked, "When are we going to write about joy?" Her question floored me. As she pointed out, I'd given them writing prompts for many different things, and we'd covered a wide range of emotional states, but none of it invited them to explore joy. Mostly we'd focused on grief, struggle, and resilience. That afternoon, I altered the agenda and we all wrote about joy. Nearly every retreat I've facilitated since has had a section dedicated to an exploration of joy.

Her question invited me to start examining my relationship with joy. Why did I make it such a low priority? Why did I find it more important to write about other things? Was I afraid to embrace it? What was on my Velcro dress that was telling me that struggle and grief were more important than joy?

WHEN I started writing this book, I thought it would be a book about the transition I was entering into at the time, launching my daughters into the world and packing up my belongings to set out in search of a new home. I'd written the allegory about the girl in the Velcro dress a few years earlier, but I didn't know she'd show up in this book until she unexpectedly met me in Costa Rica, and the book changed. Suddenly, the book was about unravelling old stories and healing trauma so that I could move into this new chapter of my life with less weight attached to my dress.

When I went to Costa Rica in the spring, it was an act of pure joy and the success of that decision helped me see other choices in the same light. At the time, I knew I wanted to spend two weeks writing, preferably somewhere away from home, and when I wasn't accepted into a writing residency I'd applied for, I reached out to my friend Mary who owns a farm and runs a school for teachers there. She'd already been thinking about inviting me, so there was no hesitancy in her generous invitation. I made plans and booked a ticket.

At the edge of Mary's farm is a river, and just above that river, she's built a "rancho"—a large shelter that houses an outdoor living room and kitchen. This is the space she gave me to write for two weeks. I was surrounded by lush green jungle and the babbling river flowed within sight of where I wrote. The cicadas sang a daily song and sometimes butterflies or birds perched on the railing that overlooked the river.

During my time there, the rancho became for me the House That Tenderness Built. It gave me boundaries and safety and kept me dry during the rainy days. It held me while I processed hard things from my past and didn't judge me when I cried. It offered me a variety of spaces for doing the work—a big soft chair when I needed coziness, a hard-back chair when I needed more structure, a dance floor when I needed to move, a cool spot on the floor near the railing where I could catch the most breeze during the hottest parts of the day, and a kitchen where I could prepare tea or pour a glass of water.

Mary and the people who work for her participated in making that a tender, supportive space for me, just the way good community does. They cheerfully brought me lunch and yummy snacks nearly every day, and I felt loved and cared for. Mary's massage therapist gave me a luxurious massage in the space nearest the river, where I could listen to the sounds of the water and the birds while my body was tenderly cared for.

In case I'm painting it as some kind of utopia, though, let me share another piece of the picture that made me chuckle. There's a storage room off the kitchen that houses the fridge. The first day I opened that door to get a cold drink, a bat swooped through my hair and into the room, joining the two others flying around the small space. They'd taken up residence in the storage room, and any time I wanted a refreshing beverage from the fridge, I had to face the bats. I gave myself a little pep talk before braving that room.

You see the metaphor I'm going for here, right? Even a perfect house, where Tenderness lives and makes the rules, still might have a dark room where you have to face the shadow. Even after all this work, I still have spaces in my life that are scary for me to enter.

I learned to live with the bats over those two weeks and if I'd stayed longer, I'd be able to enter that room as casually as Mary does. A few days after discovering them, one flew over my head as I was sitting in my cool spot on the floor, and I just smiled. We get used to our bats when we don't let them control our lives. I enjoyed cold drinks every day because I didn't let the bats stop me.

Now, as I write this, several months have passed and I am in Spain, in an equally beautiful place, putting the finishing touches on this book before I send it off to my publisher. Again, I have chosen to immerse myself in beauty, tenderness, and joy. Last week, Mary spent the week with me here in Spain and we enjoyed each other's company and the slow pace of this lovely resort town. Every day before I write, I go for long walks, and then when I need a break from the writing, I go for a swim. It feels decadent in a way I've rarely allowed myself to be decadent.

This experience, finishing my book in these beautiful places that I chose simply because I knew they would bring me joy and tenderness and I'd be well supported by people who care about me, has been good for me as I continue to lean into the decision about what's next in my life. While in Costa Rica, back in the spring, I made a joy list. I wrote down the things that will bring me joy if they are available to me in my future home and life. The list includes things like "I want to be close to water" and "I want to be near people who are safe and trustworthy." These things have been true of this beautiful place in Spain just as they were in Costa Rica.

This is how I intend to make decisions in the future—with joy as my guide and tenderness as my host. Wherever I go, I intend to seek water, kindness, and safety for my long-activated nervous system.

I am not a martyr anymore, nor am I attached to the struggle. I don't believe my Mennonite ancestors truly want me to be, now that they are free of their earthly burdens. I choose to believe that death liberated them from the trauma that shaped their lives and now they want me to continue to liberate myself and to seek more joy. I do not need to stay in situations that cause me harm. I do not need to prove my worthiness through struggle, or measure the worth of my body by capitalist yard-sticks. I am inherently worthy of love, kindness, and joy. When I receive that love and kindness, and give it generously to myself, I can more freely give it away. Everyone benefits when I surround myself with joy and tenderness.

On my way to Costa Rica last spring, after spending a few days with Nicole in Toronto, I passed through Union Station and saw a public art exhibit, by Lan "Florence" Yee, that made me catch my breath. A large poster on a pillar held these words: "Seeking a ticket to the place she feels safest." I believe that's the quest I've been on my whole life without knowing I was on it. Since the moment just after I entered the world, when my mom's heart stopped beating and her arms were subsequently pinned to the bed, I have been seeking a ticket to a place I feel safest. I denied myself that place far too many times because I didn't believe it was mine to ask for, and because the trauma and social conditioning in my body insisted on creating struggle instead of safety. I accepted a lack of safety as my birthright and perhaps my punishment.

It's taken me a long time to find it, but now I believe the safe place that I was seeking is within me, in the House That Tenderness Built. I will not exile myself from that place ever again, nor will I let anyone in who doesn't honour it. I have invested too much in it.

Now that my body finally feels safer (and when she doesn't feel safe I'm better at soothing her and creating boundaries to protect her), I will turn to my next pursuit: Joy. Whatever happens next, I will choose joy. I will lean into the practices that help me orient my life toward joy. Two of those practices have been inspired by others—witnessing my "joy triggers" and seeking out my "joy people." To those I have added two more—finding my "joy places" and doing my "joy work."

Dr. Robin Youngson, a trauma specialist whom I interviewed for one of my online courses, first inspired me to consider my joy triggers. "Although we encode trauma from our early childhood," Dr. Youngson said, "we also encode pleasure. So the moment I jump on my bicycle, I just feel joyous. As a small child, one of my earliest escapes from a difficult life was to jump on my bicycle and go off into the woods and be by myself. And that feeling has been encoded and hardwired into my brain... The moment I jump on my bicycle, my brain thinks, 'Okay, you're a happy ten-year-old boy now.'" Since that conversation, I've been paying attention to what triggers joy in my body (dancing, swimming, hiking, woodworking, art-making, travelling), and I've been seeking more of that.

My friend Desiree Adaway was the first person I heard use the term "joy people." When Desiree and I were both in the fledgling stages of building our businesses, I was lamenting how much, as an introvert, I hated going to networking events, where everyone is polite and overly friendly and the goal is to get your business card into the most hands. "You're going about it all wrong," Desiree said, in her direct but loving way. "Instead of 'networking,' you have to go out there and seek out your 'joy people.' Go to those events where the kind of people who bring you joy will gather and skip the rest." Ever since then, I've been intentionally gathering joy people around me, and that's how I've built my business. These aren't necessarily people who are always joyful (that would be tiresome), but those who are most likely to spark joy in me just by their presence.

As for my "joy places"—well, that's fairly self-explanatory. Especially now, after selling my house and setting off on a personal quest that's taking me to various places in the world, I'm paying attention to the places that spark the most joy in me. I am partial to bodies of water—especially an ocean or sea. I also like little Spanish towns that have a fun vibe and queer-friendly beaches. And places with large trees—redwoods or palm trees. And quirky little islands where signs are hand-painted and eggs are bought on the honour system from a cooler at the end of a driveway.

Finally, my "joy work." As I finish writing this book, I can say, unequivocally, that writing is my primary joy work. That doesn't mean that it always brings me joy—far from it; it can be excruciating sometimes—but it consistently brings me enough joy that I keep coming back to the page. Teaching and hosting meaningful conversation circles and retreats also bring me joy. I have found, in fact, that the best way for me to find joy in my work is to mix things up—to sometimes be doing introverted writing where I hide away from people for a few weeks at a time, and sometimes be doing more extroverted teaching or facilitating where I'm in conversation most of the time.

The kind of joy that I'm seeking is not a superficial joy. I'm talking about the kind of deep, embodied joy that knows how to live side by side with melancholy, grief, and disappointment without needing to chase any emotions away. As Walt Whitman wrote, "I am large. I contain multitudes."

Whenever the old stories rise up and I am tempted to sabotage my joy, I try to remember to stand in the waves and trust that joy is available to me there. I breathe deeply and tell my body that she is safe, just as she was safe in that rancho near the river, even when the bats flew over my head, and just as she is safe in a queer-friendly town on the Mediterranean Sea where I walked along the shore to the clothing optional beach, took off my clothes, and dove into the waves naked. When I forget that my body is safe, I will reach out to the people who know how to remind me. If absolutely necessary (or even simply desired), I will fly to Costa Rica or Spain for a reminder.

I didn't expect Joy to come today
In the middle of this week spent mostly with Melancholy,
But there she was, tapping on my car window,
In the Shoppers Drug Mart parking lot.

The sun peeked from behind the cloud and lit her face
As she climbed into the passenger seat of my car.
"You don't have to go back to work just yet," she said.
"Let's go to the beach and play."

Reason tried to convince her there were Important Things
That I needed to do, back at the office,
But she laughed at me and said,
"Well, I have Important Things to do at the beach."

"Your work can wait for another day.
The beach, though? It can't wait," she said.
"The days will get colder soon,
And then you'll be sorry you missed it."

I turned the car toward the beach and she squealed her
    delight.
But then, because I let her have that one win, she started get-
    ting bossy.
"You let Melancholy pick the playlist," she said, with a grimace.
She grabbed my phone to load her own playlist and
I knew there was no point in arguing.

We car-danced our way to the beach.
Once there, Joy insisted that I play in the waves with her,
Even though the water was cold.
We waded in until our rolled-up pants were soaking wet,

And then we talked to seagulls, wrote our names in the sand,
And gathered shells and bits of sea glass.

"These are the Important Things
We needed to do today," Joy said,
"Because life is better with sea glass and sandy toes."
(She's a bit obnoxious when she's right.)

At the end of the day,
The sun winked at us
And then settled into the trees at the edge of the beach.
Once her painted pinks and oranges
Had faded from the sky,
We turned back to our car and headed home.

"You were good company today," Joy said softly,
As she snuggled into my passenger seat,
Closed her eyes,
And drifted off to sleep.

REFLECTION QUESTIONS

THE HEALING WORK that I've written about in this book has allowed me to arrive at the place where I am now, more fully embracing joy and allowing joy to be the guiding light for my life. I do not expect to always be joyful, but I no longer run away from joy (in fact, I actively seek it out). I've learned to hold space for it in the same way that I hold space for other emotions. Reflect on your own relationship with joy and whether or not you feel ready to embrace it and actively seek it out.

1   What is your relationship with joy? Do you embrace it? Do you worship it? Do you ignore it? Do you sabotage it? Do you hold space for it?

2   What do you want to change about your relationship with joy?

3   Some of my response to joy was rooted in a body that didn't feel safe in the world. How safe do you feel? Do you frequently notice that your nervous system is activated? If you don't feel safe, what might help you get closer to that?

4   I wrote about a sign I saw in Toronto: "Seeking a ticket to the place she feels safest." If you were to create a similar art piece, what would it say after "Seeking"?

5   Consider what things trigger joy in your body. Make a list of joy triggers. What will you do to more actively seek out and embrace joy?

6   Who are your "joy people"?

7   Where are your "joy places"?

8   What's your "joy work"?

EPILOGUE
The Girl in the Painted Dress

AFTER MANY pieces had been removed, the girl saw that the dress was becoming transformed. Where the Velcro had worn away, the dress was translucent and, from the underside, paintings were showing through. At first, this made her feel too exposed, and so she hid those exposed bits and only uncovered them in the privacy of her own home. But whenever she looked in the mirror, she noticed how happy those painted bits made her feel, and so she took some chances and left the house with nothing covering the paintings.

Some people, whose clothes were heavy with Velcro bits, looked at her in shock and disapproval when they saw her exposed paintings. But others, whose clothes were lighter, like hers, smiled and winked at her. When she paused to look at who was smiling, she realized that many of them were her friends from the magical room. They looked a little different when they were walking around outside the magical room, in the common spaces where their Velcro clothing was still culturally expected, but she could see the familiar awakeness in their eyes and in their bodies.

Some of them had paintings showing through their clothing as well and some, inspired by her courage, let their coverings slip to the floor. They grinned at each other when this happened, enjoying the messy imperfection of it all.

The girl began to polish her paintings and add flourishes and sparkle. In the spots where she applied extra sparkle, nothing could stick to the dress and that filled her with even more courage and delight.

The more colourful and sparkly the dress became and the fewer bits attached to it, the more she was able to move freely in the world. She discovered that she loved the way the colourful dress flowed around her as she danced and twirled. Whenever she moved like that, people were drawn to the girl in the painted dress. They would stand and watch her, and when she paused to look at them, she recognized the longing in the eyes of those whose Velcro clothing was still heavy with attachments. It was the same longing she'd had before she'd discovered the secret cave under her dress.

Sometimes those with heavy Velcro clothing would ask, "How did you learn to do that?" Whenever they did, the girl would lean in and whisper, "Slip down under your stiff clothing and see what you find there." The people would look at her in wonder and she'd smile at them and encourage them to try. Sometimes they would scoff at her and walk away shaking their heads, but sometimes she could tell by the light in their eyes that they would go home and find a private place to try. For those whose eyes lit up, she would lean in a second time and say, "Once you've been there for a while, and you've worked up some courage, find the little door at the bottom, go through it, and I'll meet you in the magical room on the other side."

That was how the girl in the painted dress found a new source of courage and began to gather people around her. She built a whole new life for herself, teaching other people how to free themselves from their own Velcro clothing and how to stop getting attached to other people's baggage. Her painted dress was never perfect, and sometimes things still stuck to her, especially when she was tired, anxious, or lonely, but it became easier and easier to let those things go.

Early in the peeling process, she imagined someday she'd be free, that there would one day be nothing but glitter, paint, and lightness. But somewhere along the line, she stopped believing that that was the point of the exercise because even that expectation, in a strange way, was a piece attached to her dress.

Instead of hanging on to a vision of a perfect dress, she came to see that the work was about loving herself more fully, no matter what was still clinging to the dress, no matter how imperfect it all looked, and no matter how many scars there were. There was paint in some spots and Velcro bits still in others, and she practiced loving the whole imperfect mess. She realized, in fact, that some of the bits of Velcro were worth keeping because they connected her back to her lineage and, when she'd learned to love those bits, they'd become beautiful.

The girl knew she lived in an imperfect world that still made it impossible to live without Velcro clothing, so she learned to accept what was there while still working to change what she could.

When she could look in the mirror with less shame and more tenderness, the girl could see others that way too, and that felt good. She never stopped peeling. There were always new ways in which she wanted to evolve, but she let go of an image of what a perfect dress (or body beneath it) would look like. She let go of an expectation about what freedom would feel like. She let go, and she leaned into the life she had—with courage and with joy.

Final Reflection

ONCE YOU have completed the book and worked your way through the reflection questions after each chapter, take some time to do one (or all) of the following completion exercises:

- Write a letter to your past selves, promising you will do your best to hold space and heal whatever they bring (or have already brought) to your attention.

- Make an item of Velcro clothing and attach things to it and then consider what you're ready to peel off. You can make it out of cloth or Velcro, or you can draw it on a large piece of paper and use sticky notes to represent the bits attached to the clothing.

- Write a letter to your future self, making whatever commitments you need to make about what you will do in the coming weeks, months, and years to work on your healing and liberation.

- Write a Tenderness and Liberation Manifesto, listing all the ways in which you will intentionally bring more of these things into your life.

- Create a visual representation of the House That Tenderness Built. (You can do this as a collage or find a container that you fill with special things.) Consider all the things you want more of your life—things that will support you in being more tender with yourself.

Acknowledgements

FIRST, TO the people who shaped me, especially in my early days—Mom and Dad—thank you for your imperfect offering and, most of all, for your love. Then, to the people who shared my early experiences most closely—my siblings Brad, Dwight, and Cynthia—thank you for travelling with me.

Thank you, as well, to all my Mennonite foremothers and forefathers. It wasn't always easy growing up Mennonite, but there are many things I continue to be grateful for. You lived your values and faith with integrity and courage, and you forged a path for me.

To my daughters, who survived the early fumbling years of my motherhood, who challenged me, healed with me, and continue to believe in me—thank you, Nicole, Julie, and Madeline.

To my business partner, who has an unwavering faith in my ability to write and create new things, who picks up a lot of slack so that I can disappear when I need to write, and who believes with me in the possibilities for our healing and growth to contribute to a better world—thank you, Krista.

To my teaching team who, along with Krista, took on the bulk of the online teaching work this year so that I could focus on completing this work—thank you to Emily, Mary, and Nam (and welcome to Iván and Lucy). (Thank you to past members of the team as well.)

To my learning community—all of you who engage in the work we offer through the Centre for Holding Space—thank you for showing up and supporting this work so that it can grow.

To my friends who hold me up when I'm wobbly, who encourage me when the writing gets hard, who laugh with me when life feels ridiculous, and who keep showing up for the messy bits—thank you. You are too many to name. (A special shout out—because they are the ones whose stories appear on the pages of this book—to Saleha and Randy.)

To the variety of therapists, workshop/retreat facilitators, body workers, and other healers who have helped me find a way to move through the pain to the other side—thank you. (You know who you are.)

To my publishing team at Page Two—Trena, who was a champion for this book from the moment we first spoke about it; Kendra, whose editorial prowess made my words even better; Adrineh, who kept the process on track; Meghan, who started thinking up marketing ideas almost before the ink on the contract was dry; Taysia, whose design is on these pages; and Melissa, who did careful line editing.

Notes

Preface

p. 1   *writing and rewriting our stories of pain:* Daniel J. Siegel, *Mindsight: The New Science of Personal Transformation* (Bantam, 2010).

p. 2   *As Joni Mitchell has said of her songs:* Joni Mitchell quoted in *Joni Mitchell: 50 Years of Blue* (BBC Two, 2021).

1: The Woman I Needed Her to Be

p. 21   *A healing fantasy is the kind of hopeful story:* Lindsay C. Gibson, *Adult Children of Emotionally Immature Parents: How to Heal from Distant, Rejecting, or Self-Involved Parents* (New Harbinger Publications, 2015).

2: His Hands at My Throat

p. 35   *It can seem perplexing from the outside:* Sarah Polley, *Run Towards the Danger: Confrontations with a Body of Memory* (Hamish Hamilton, 2022).

p. 36   *"Although fight-or-flight may characterize:* Shelley E. Taylor et al., "Biobehavioral Responses to Stress in Females: Tend-and-Befriend, Not Fight-or-Flight," *Psychological Review* 107, no.3 (2000), doi.org/10.1037/0033-295X.107.3.411. See also Shelley E. Taylor, "Tend and Befriend Theory," in *Handbook of Theories of Social Psychology*, vol. 1, ed. Paul A.M. Van Lange et al. (Sage Publications, 2012).

p. 43   *"Perhaps all the dragons in our lives:* Rainer Maria Rilke, *Letters to a Young Poet,* trans. Charlie Louth (Penguin Classics, 2014).

3: Faith and Flotation

p. 50   *"Why would they need counselling:* Linda Pressly, "The Rapes Haunting a Community That Shuns the 21st Century," BBC News, May 16, 2019, bbc.com/news/stories-48265703.

p. 51   *"Our ministers always say we have to forgive:* Pressly, "The Rapes Haunting a Community."

p. 52   *impact of trauma on Mennonite women who fled Stalinist Russia*: Elizabeth Krahn, "An Autoethnographic Study of the Legacies of Collective Trauma Experienced by Russian Mennonite Women Who Immigrated to Canada After WWII: Implications on Aging and the Next Generation," master's thesis, University of Manitoba, 2011, mspace.lib.umanitoba.ca/server/api/core/bitstreams/d6037a99 -eed7-4ab9-952a-683838ad5a9a/content.

p. 62   *"A rigid religion fosters dependency:* Marlene Winell, *Leaving the Fold: A Guide for Former Fundamentalists and Others Leaving Their Religion* (Apocryphile Press, 2006).

p. 65   *the response in Manitoba to the COVID-19 pandemic:* Ian Froese, "This Manitoba Community Has a Vaccination Rate of 24% Against COVID-19. Here's Why," CBC News, September 29, 2021, cbc.ca/news/ canada/manitoba/manitoba-covid-19-stanley-winkler-morden- southern-health-wfpcbc-cbc-1.6192673.

p. 65   *"could not stay away from the place of execution: The Bloody Theatre, or Martyrs Mirror of the Defenseless Christians, Who Baptized Only upon Confession of Faith, and Who Suffered and Died for the Testimony of Jesus, Their Savior, from the Time of Christ to the Year A.D. 1660,* 5th ed., compiled by Thieleman J. van Braght, trans. Joseph F. Sohm (Herald Press, 1950).

4: The Woman Behind the Door

p. 84   *codependency is "a dysfunctional relationship dynamic:* "Codependency," *Psychology Today,* psychologytoday.com/ca/basics/ codependency.

p. 85   *Ever since people first existed:* Melody Beattie, *Codependent No More: How to Stop Controlling Others and Start Caring for Yourself* (Hazelden, 1986).

p. 85   *Dr. Stephen Karpman's Drama Triangle:* Wikipedia, s.v. "Karpman Drama Triangle," en.wikipedia.org/wiki/Karpman_drama_triangle.

p. 86   *a new triangle where the victim becomes the creator:* David Emerald, *The Power of TED: The Empowerment Dynamic,* 10th anniversary ed. (Polaris Publishing, 2017).

5: This Fat Body

p. 109   *"Living in a female body:* Sonya Renee Taylor, *The Body Is Not an Apology: The Power of Radical Self-Love,* 2nd ed. (Berrett-Koehler Publishers, 2021).

p. 111   *"Saying I'm fat is (and should be):* Taylor, *The Body Is Not an Apology.*

6: Intersections

p. 119   *These evolved in response to an article in* Maclean's *magazine:* Nancy Macdonald, "Welcome to Winnipeg: Where Canada's Racism Problem Is at Its Worst," *Maclean's,* January 22, 2015, macleans.ca/news/canada/welcome-to-winnipeg-where-canadas-racism-problem-is-at-its-worst/.

p. 121   *During the Middle Ages in Europe:* Resmaa Menakem, "Healing Your Thousand-Year-Old Trauma," Medium, June 7, 2018, medium.com/@rmenakem/healing-our-thousand-year-old-trauma-d815009ae93.

p. 124   *"a lens through which you can see where power comes and collides:* Kimberlé Crenshaw quoted in "Kimberlé Crenshaw on Intersectionality, More Than Two Decades Later," Columbia Law School, June 8, 2017, law.columbia.edu/news/archive/kimberle-crenshaw-intersectionality-more-two-decades-later.

p. 125   *"An ally will mostly engage in activism:* Colleen Clemens, "Ally or Accomplice? The Language of Activism," Learning for Justice, June 5, 2017, learningforjustice.org/magazine/ally-or-accomplice-the-language-of-activism.

p. 127   *"Radical self-love summons us to be:* Sonya Renee Taylor, *The Body Is Not an Apology: The Power of Radical Self-Love,* 2nd ed. (Berrett-Koehler Publishers, 2021).

7: Power Tools and Paintbrushes

p. 137 *May this home be a place of discovery:* John O'Donohue, "For a New Home," in *To Bless the Space Between Us: A Book of Blessings* (Doubleday, 2008).

8: The Value of a Home

p. 155 *"Think of body shame like:* Sonya Renee Taylor, *The Body Is Not an Apology: The Power of Radical Self-Love,* 2nd ed. (Berrett-Koehler Publishers, 2021).

12: Embracing Joy

p. 211 *As Walt Whitman wrote:* Walt Whitman, "Song of Myself, 51," in *Leaves of Grass* (First Avenue Editions, 1892).

CHANTELLE DIONE PHOTOGRAPHY

About the Author

HEATHER PLETT is an international speaker, facilitator, and author of the award-winning book *The Art of Holding Space*. She is also the co-founder of the Centre for Holding Space, where she has mentored an international team of people to deliver online and in-person workshops based on her work. Internationally known as a leading expert on the practice of holding space, Heather's work has been referenced in publications such as the *Harvard Business Review*, the *Daily Beast*, and *Psychology Today*, and has been included in curricula for nurses, hospice care workers, yoga teachers, death doulas, and military chaplains.

Let's Keep the Conversation Going

THANK YOU for reading *Where Tenderness Lives: On Healing, Liberation, and Holding Space for Oneself.* I would love to hear your feedback. Please share your thoughts on social media using the following hashtags and handle: **#wheretendernesslives · #heatherplett #holdingspace · @heatherplett** (on most social media platforms)

If you enjoyed this book, please consider writing a review on the platform of your choosing. Your feedback is incredibly valuable for helping independent authors like me to reach a wider audience.

You can find more of my writing on my personal blog, **heatherplett.com**, and you can find the courses I've developed (together with my business partner, Krista dela Rosa) at **centreforholdingspace.com**.